Photographs that make you think.

AF400722

HUMANS

Henry Carroll

ABRAMS IMAGE, NEW YORK

CONTENTS

8 BODY

MARIA KOKUNOVA · MARK McKNIGHT · GLENDA LISSETTE
ISABELLE WENZEL · KATE PETERS · MARI KATAYAMA
PAUL MPAGI SEPUYA · CASSILS · CARA PHILLIPS · MAIJA TAMMI

42 FAITH

ANA ZIBELNIK · KHADIJA SAYE · DAVID AVAZZADEH
ALYS TOMLINSON · PAWEL JASZCZUK · MARWAN BASSIOUNI
KRISTINE POTTER · MURRAY BALLARD

66 CONNECTION

LINDLEY WARREN MICKUNAS · MASAKI YAMAMOTO
JONNY BRIGGS · PIXY LIAO · LUIS ALBERTO RODRIGUEZ
ANDRES GONZALEZ · GEORGE GEORGIOU
JACK DAVISON · DEANNA DIKEMAN

96
DIVISION

LAURENCE RASTI · ZANELE MUHOLI · JAMMIE HOLMES
GUANYU XU · KEYEZUA · XAVIERA SIMMONS
RYAN DEBOLSKI · DOUG RICKARD

118
CONTROL

LINDSAY GODIN · PETER FUNCH · ADJI DIEYE
SILVIA ROSI · RODRIGO VALENZUELA · ABDO SHANAN
CLÉMENT LAMBELET · AMY ELKINS

Introduction 4
Photo Credits 142
Acknowledgments 143

INTRODUCTION

Here is a certainty: In your lifetime, you will witness more rapid and fundamental changes than any other humans in the history of our species. We are, of course, the lucky ones, the ones benefiting from the accumulated knowledge and labor of the one hundred billion minds and bodies who have lived and died before. But what happens now? What happens when our constant advances see us changing the world faster than we can adapt to it? Our knowledge of medicine means that our life expectancy is now significantly longer than our bodies have evolved to withstand, and in order to go the distance, we need to be pumped with drugs and have our bones, quite literally, reinforced.

Though we are "only human" and "nobody is perfect," the acceleration of image culture has brainwashed us into accepting very specific and very narrow definitions of beauty that exclude almost everyone. At the same time, and on a weekly basis, science is providing definitive answers to questions that have preoccupied us for millennia. These answers are entirely at odds with those provided by the world's religions, yet the vast majority of us maintain an unshakable commitment to our faith and turn to it for guidance above all else. Today we are never lost, we are never out of contact with those we love; but this newfound connectivity is starting to chip away at our primal need for physical touch, for authentic interactions with people and nature. In terms of health and wealth, inequality has spiraled out of control to such an extent that death and taxes are now starting to feel like optional extras for those at the top. In the West, many of those belonging to the group that has held on to power for so long—white people—are struggling to accept that in order to achieve meaningful equality, they are going to have to share all the fruits of human endeavor. And then there is the biggie: our unrelenting and excessive levels of consumption—our desire for bigger, smaller, faster, cheaper—that is now confronting us with the possibility of our extinction. Nothing, anymore, feels permanent.

As is often the case, it takes the eyes of an outsider to see what's really going on. Unfortunately, since our own eyes are the only ones we have, we humans lack that privilege. A more advanced alien species might look at our current situation with amusement: "Behold the growing pains of a fledgling civilization!" they might gurgle. Or maybe not. Perhaps they, like many of us, would be a little nervous, a little dumbfounded by the paradox at the heart of it all: We humans have gone full throttle and created a world to suit our needs, and now we find ourselves struggling to adapt to the world we have created. And though we cannot turn to aliens for answers, we can at least turn to those of us who are dedicated to helping us see ourselves a little more clearly—namely, artists, and more specifically artists of the photographic kind, who quite literally have the power to freeze time to give us a much-needed pause for thought. Their work is confronting and instinctive. It is the product of very human humans who feel the urgency of this moment in time, a time when we must take a breath to ponder our place, as individuals and as a collective, in this strange new world.

For me, your fellow human, compiling a relatively concise book on such a gigantic subject was, of course, a daunting challenge. Even the word itself, "humans," feels a little abstract. I am a human. You are a human. We are humans. But what does that mean? What connects me to you and us to everybody else? What, if anything, is still important to us all? Though I cannot say I have arrived at the answer, I have arrived at an answer—one offered to me by the photographers featured here. Slowly, something revealed itself as I collected the work of hundreds of photographers—something I could not ignore. Using keywords to categorize their concerns, I found that one of the following five words appeared next to almost every photographer: Body, Faith, Connection, Division, and Control. It seemed that for many photographers, these areas of interest (and contention) are the kernels at the core of their reflections on humanity; and as you immerse yourselves in the images, it's my hope that you'll begin to see why.

There is something very primal, something deeply human, about these aspects of our existence, which relate to our conscious awareness of our bodies, our need to believe in something greater than ourselves, our desire for intimate human contact, our innate impulse to form and protect groups of similar individuals, and our need for social order and hierarchies of power. Yet when we perceive the world around us, it's clear that these aspects of being human have grown into societal norms that all too often put us in conflict with our primordial needs. In fact, for many, they have become entrenched systems of suppression, intolerance, and judgment. In the section entitled "Body," Mark McKnight presents us with an almost reverential gaze at male bodies that have been excluded from the parameters of beauty, while Glenda Lissette takes back control of her social media self-image through a fascinating process of digital deformation. In "Faith," David Avazzadeh reflects on the commodification of spirituality in the smartphone era, while Marwan Bassiouni shows how he quite literally finds space for his Muslim faith in the West. "Connection" features Jonny Briggs, who probes his relationship with his parents through cathartic collages, and Pixy Liao, who finds a willing muse in her longtime boyfriend in order to challenge gender roles in heterosexual relationships. In "Division," the self-portraits of Zanele Muholi and Xaviera Simmons break down stereotypical representations of Blackness and confront us with racial injustices past and present. Finally, "Control" sees Clément Lambelet co-opting facial recognition software to question a computer's ability to understand emotion, while Amy Elkins's correspondence with people on death row provides insight into the minds of incarcerated people.

Image making is, by nature, a little primitive, a little primal. Humans have been making images for more than forty thousand years, and in a way, not much has changed since then; whether stencils of hands on the wall of a cave or a collection of pixels contained in a camera phone, all images are visual responses to what is taking place around us and within us, fleeting and not-so-fleeting acknowledgments of what matters most. Another enduring aspect of images is their inherent ambiguity. On their own, images can tell us only so much, they suggest rather than explain; their meaning, their resonance, changes from one person to the next. That is why, when it comes to reflecting on the subject of humans, visual language—the primal language—is so important: To make sense of what we are seeing, we must bring ourselves to images. In other words, to form an understanding of an image is to better understand ourselves. You may not share the story of some of the image makers in this book—they might be preoccupied by themes or issues that do not concern you—but I guarantee that within each image, each idea, you will find a little something that does resonate with your own human experience. Maybe Mari Katayama's acceptance of her body will, in a small way, inspire you to accept your own. Maybe you will see yourself in one of the faces that Peter Funch photographs returning to the same spot every single day. Maybe Deanna Dikeman's archive, which spans thirty years of her parents waving good-bye to her in their driveway, will prompt you to think about who it is you photograph most often, and why.

A collection of responses. That is what we have here. Responses to a world that constantly challenges our understanding of what it means to be human—a world that is, for good or bad, giving us the opportunity to decide which parts of "human" we want to keep and which parts we are willing to let go.

BO

We have always been a little discontented with our bodies. Mechanically, our bodies tend to fail us long before our minds do, and aesthetically, we have grown more and more self-conscious or dissatisfied with the way we look. Since the discovery of antibiotics, just ninety years ago, we are now able to reach inside the human body without the risk of infection. Safe and relatively easy procedures allow us to perform "upgrades," replace faulty parts and remodel features so they conform to current beauty trends. Many of us measure what we put into our bodies down to a single calorie, or gram of protein, and expect them to function just like computers. And, of course, we now have two bodies, one real, one

We have always been a little discontented with our bodies.

virtual; the latter we can manipulate in any way we wish and control like a puppet. This relatively newfound ability to improve on what nature has given—to speed up, as it were, the evolutionary process—has led to a hyper-awareness of how we perceive our bodies and the bodies of others. This hyperawareness has also significantly influenced how the body is being represented through the camera lens. The photographers in this section delve into the physical, social, and political complexities that inform our relationship to the body. Some take their starting point from history, others break down very narrow-minded conventions to challenge long-accepted modes of representation. New visual languages are explored by those whose inquisitive gaze has been, and still is, suppressed due to race, gender, or sexuality. These photographers rally against a culture that is highly judgmental of the way we look. They expose their own desires and fears and challenge what were once regarded as concrete classifications. With honesty and directness, their work widens the definitions of beauty and ever so slightly loosens our straitjacketed conception of what is and isn't physically acceptable.

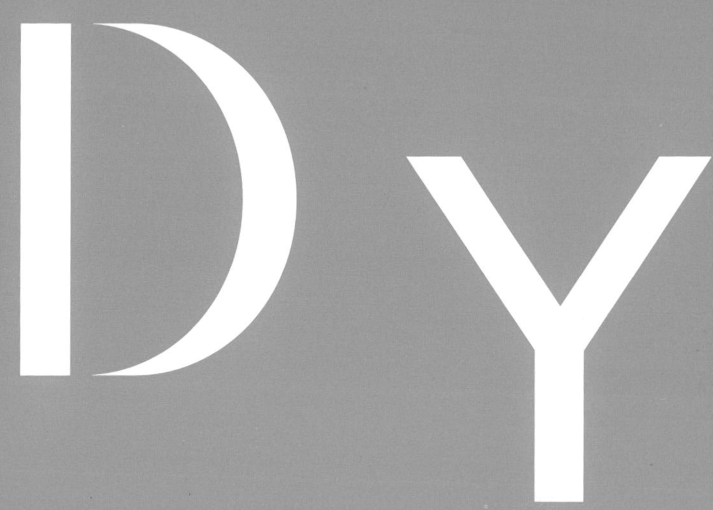

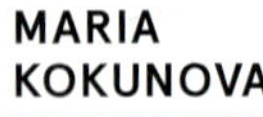

**MARIA
KOKUNOVA**

Do you live inside your body?

The French psychoanalyst Jacques Lacan theorized that the moment one recognizes oneself in the mirror as an infant, that sudden self-awareness plants a seed in one's mind that leads to a lifelong struggle with identity. The face in the mirror is mine, but it does not represent the complexities of what's beneath the surface—of how I feel, of the true workings of my consciousness. If I cannot recognize myself in myself, how is anyone else supposed to truly understand me? In her series *Face*, Maria Kokunova delves into the psychological disconnection between mind, body, and vision. Her photographs often fixate on the hands, the go-to body parts when it comes to searching for answers about ourselves. Our fingerprints, for example, are unique, and palmistry seeks meaning in the patterns on our palms in the form of life-, heart-, and head-line readings. Seeing her body through her eyes intensifies Kokunova's inward gaze. Her eyes become the camera, like we are inside her head. By focusing attention on the minutiae of her physical being, from the lines on her hands to the moment of cutting a fingernail, these self-portraits feel both intimate and alien. What should we make of the subtle deviations of symmetry on our palms? How do we relate to the crescent of our clipped nail? Through these concentrated moments of bodily self-analysis, Kokunov raises a very human quandary when it comes to our relationship with our physical selves, one that is complicated by our highly developed consciousness; when I look at myself, whether in the mirror or down at my hands, who is this "me" who seems to exist both inside and outside my body?

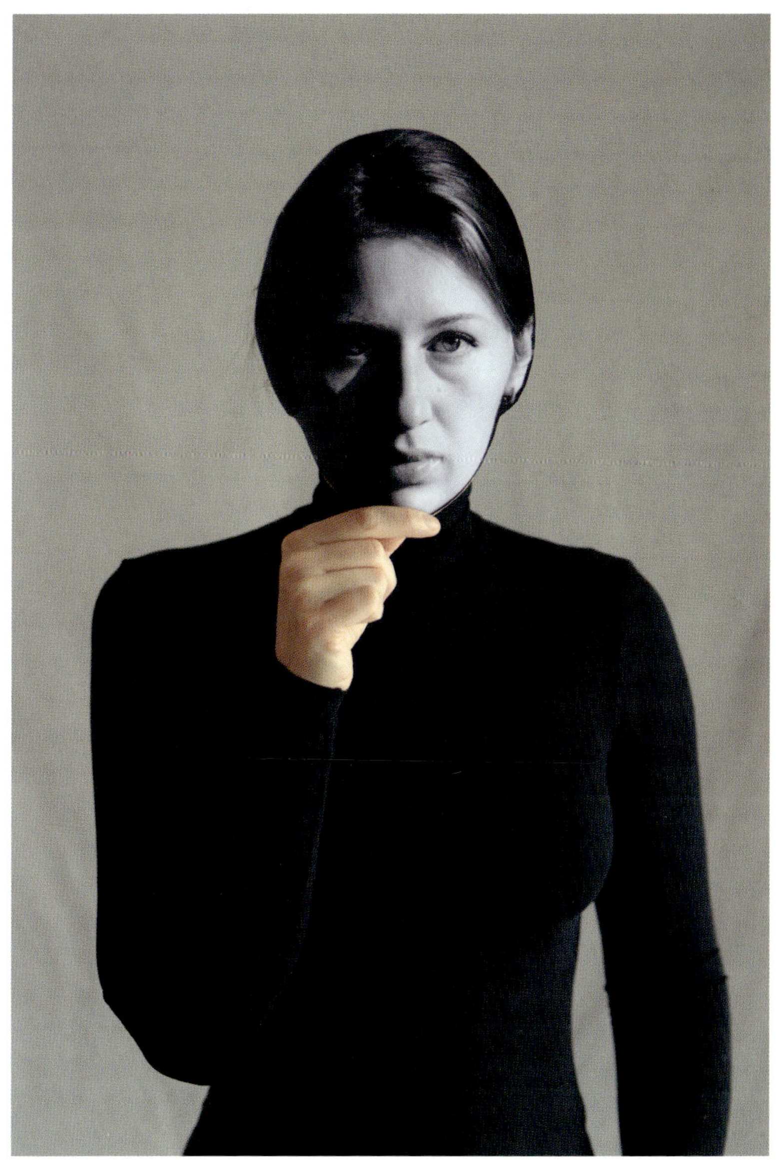

Above and following spread: Untitled, from the series Face, 2018

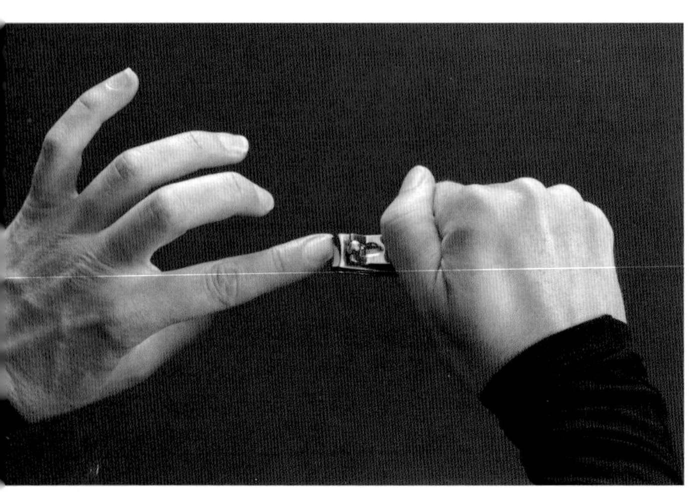

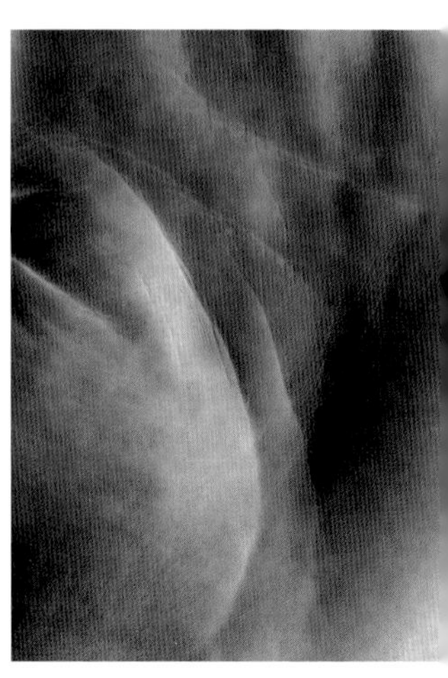

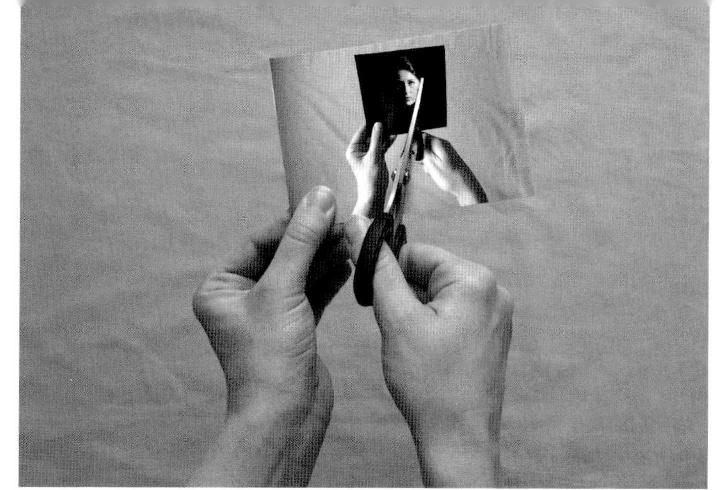

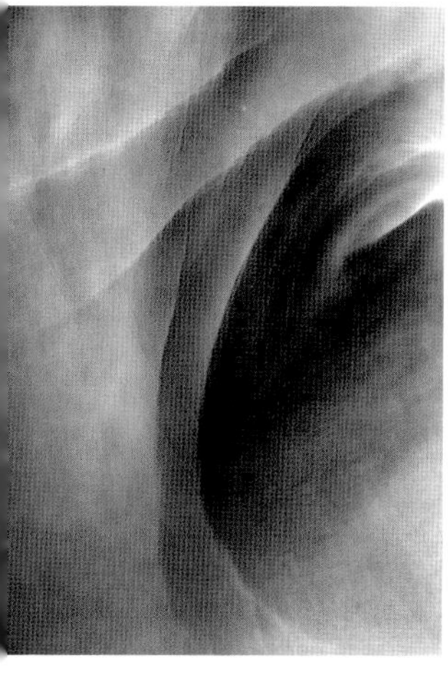

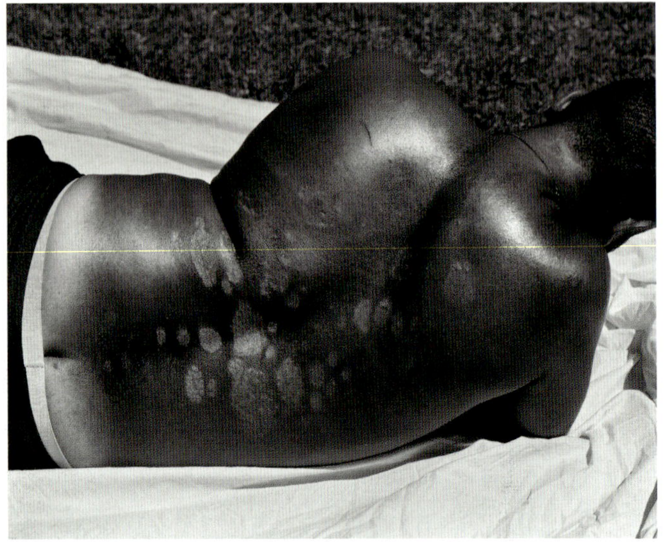

Who is photo-genic?

Environmental forms become entwined with the dark-skinned bodies of the Los Angeles queer community in Mark McKnight's series *Decreation*. Violence and tenderness coalesce to create intimate studies of socially, politically, and aesthetically "imperfect" bodies, the kind of bodies excluded from the historical canon of photography, which has been defined largely by the eyes of straight, white men. The scarred flesh on a man's back invites comparisons to a gashed sack of gravel or the shapes of oil swirls on water; corpulent limbs covered in thick, dark body hair are equated visually to weathered stone and cracked concrete; holes

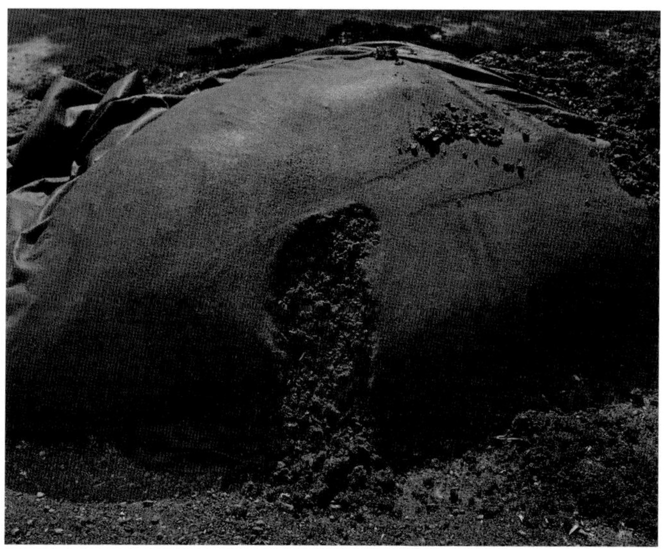

in hard rock appear libidinous. To sum it up neatly, one could say that McKnight's work reminds us that no matter who we desire, our bodies are products of nature and are all therefore equally deserving of attention. But McKnight's gaze is a little more complex, a little less literal than that. In his dark, dense prints, shadow and light both reveal and conceal. His compositions create lyrical geometries whereby a photographic fusing, or healing, takes place between opposing physical forms—soft and hard, straight and curved, textured and smooth. This intimate, sexually charged, almost reverential gaze results in a brooding beauty that calls for a new appreciation or acceptance of the male body in all its incarnations.

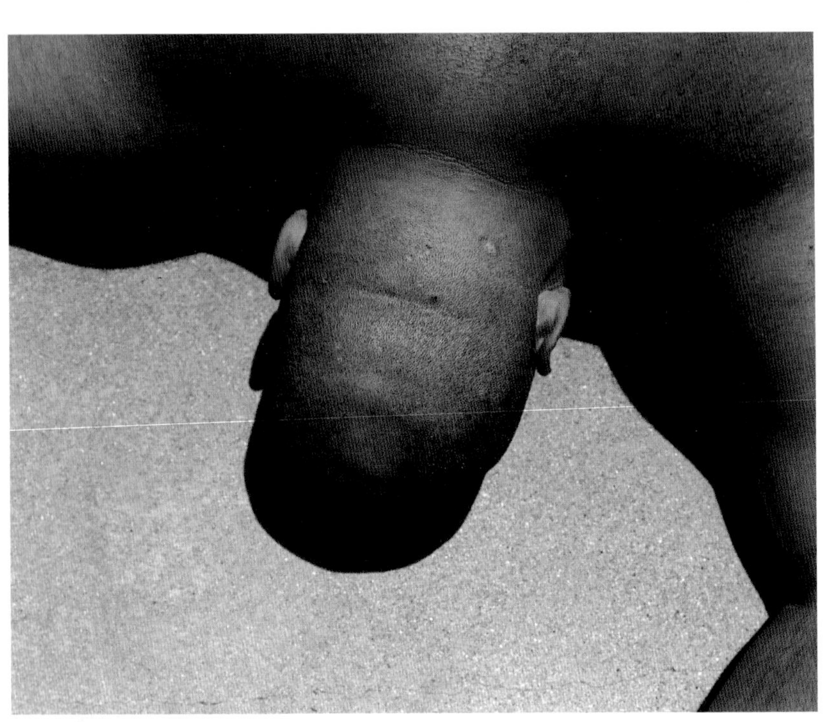

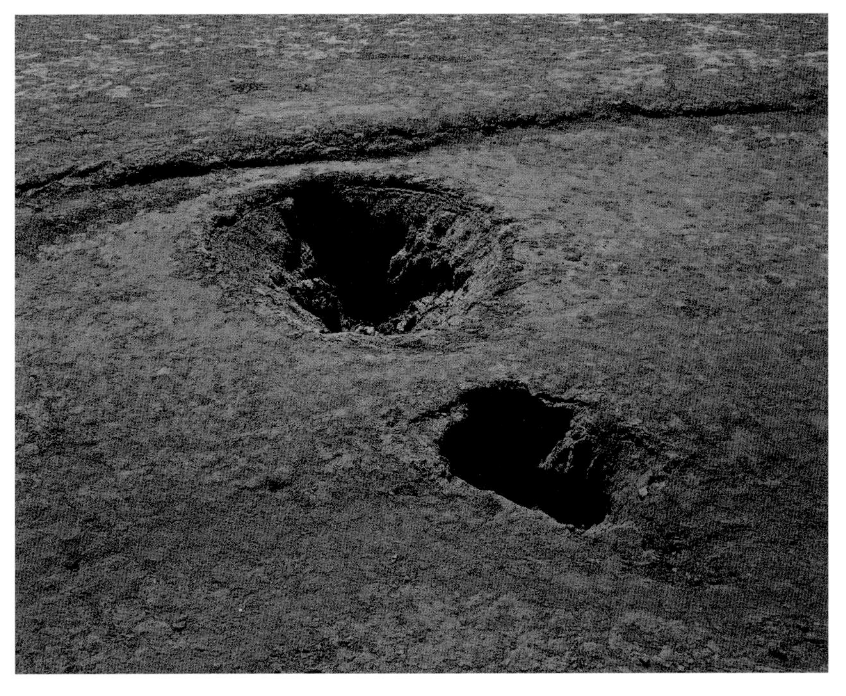

Opposite: Ballerino, 2018 | Above: Earthskin, 2018

Who is the creator of your self-image?

As a teen, Glenda Lissette started posting selfies on various social media platforms. Her images conformed to prevailing trends of female beauty online, and before long, her following grew and brands started to view her as an influencer. However, rather than succumbing to the expectations imposed on young women in order to become influencers, Lissette began using digital manipulation to deconstruct her body image. Here, the components of her pose are typical of a young, female social media influencer: supercilious expression, smooth skin, glossy lips, heavy eyeshadow, and long, flowing hair. Yet her digitally deformed arm and gangly fingers undercut this familiar visual language to transform her body into something grotesque. Her fingers grow like roots around another common influencer motif, succulents, and the way the bowl is tilted forward echoes historical "peasantry" paintings that depict women hard at work in subservient roles, such as Vincenzo Campi's *The Fruit Seller* (1580).

Of course, the brands and many followers initially drawn to Lissette's feed quickly moved on to claim and control the bodies of other young women. This has left Lissette occupying a space in which she harnesses the power of the platform to deconstruct the toxicity of the digital world it has created. Yet hers is not a position of opposition to, or ridicule of, female influencers. By manipulating her own body, in playing the role of "influencer" on her own terms, Lissette demonstrates the empowerment that comes with being in control of one's self-image in an arena where gender roles are often as entrenched as those of the peasant women of bygone days.

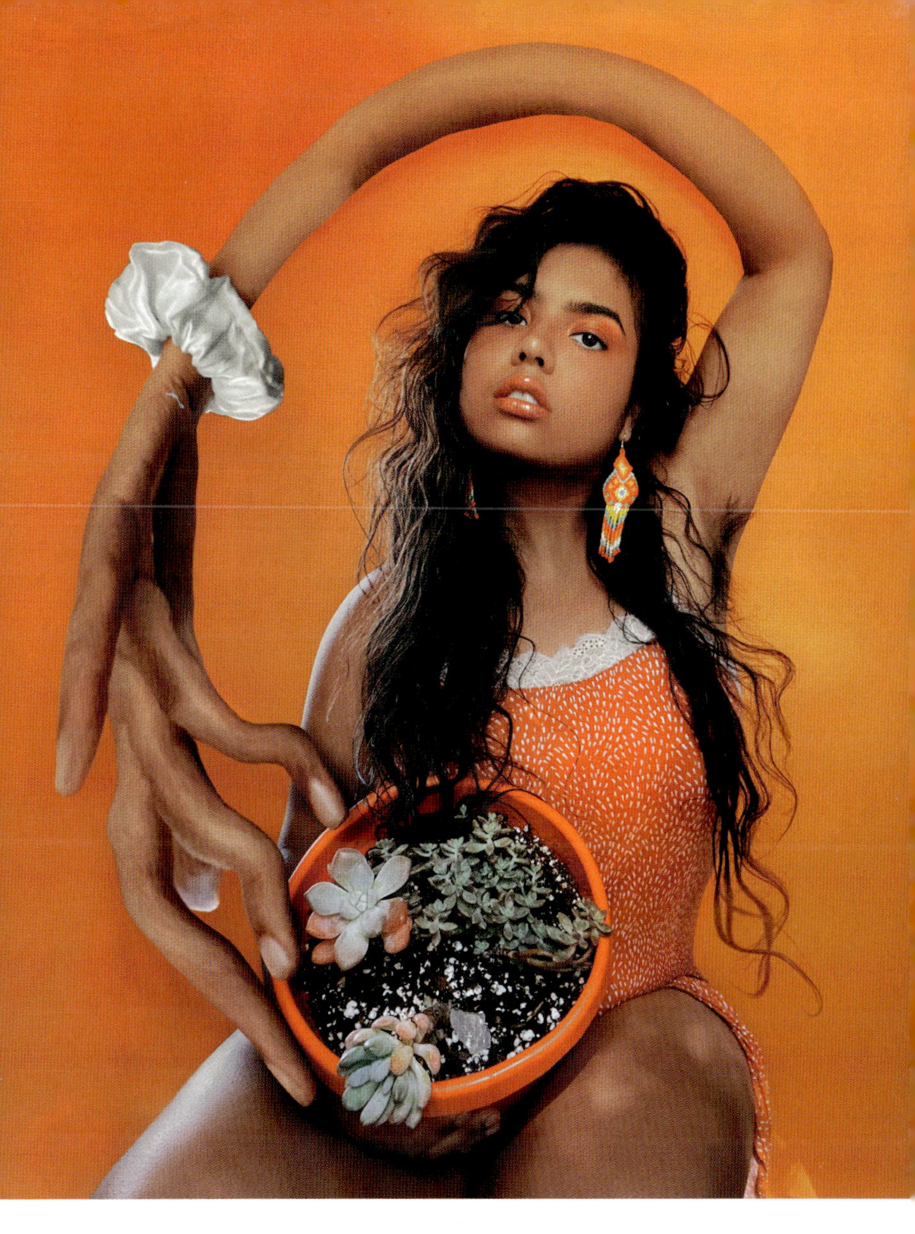

Think I Fight Demons When I Sleep Because I Wake Up with Tight Hands, July 6, 2020

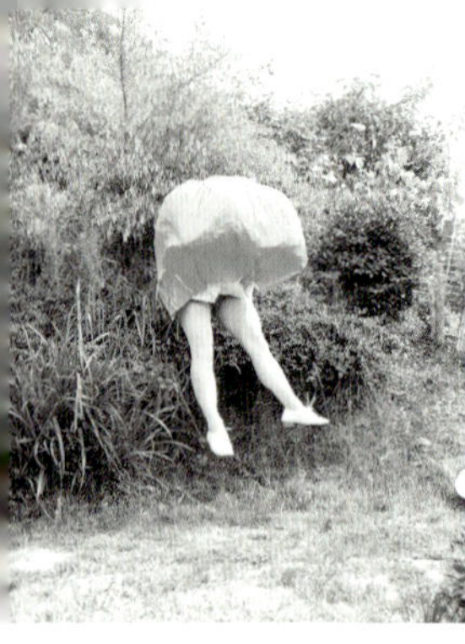
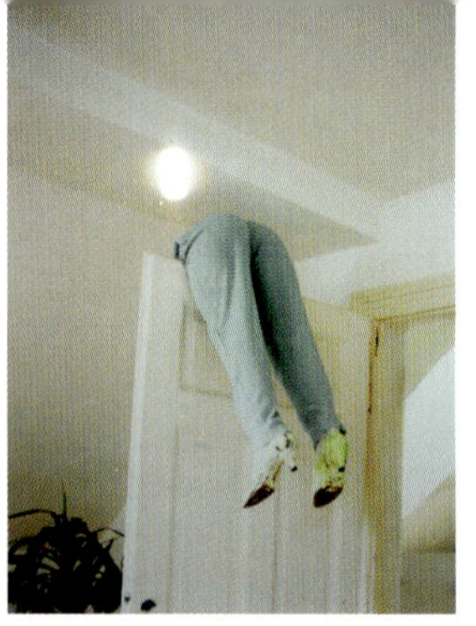
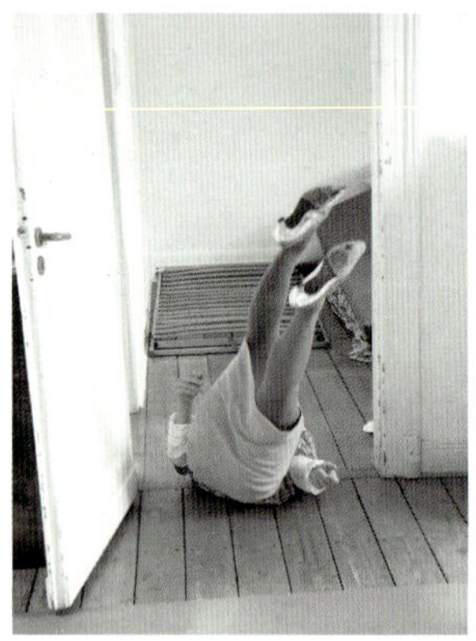
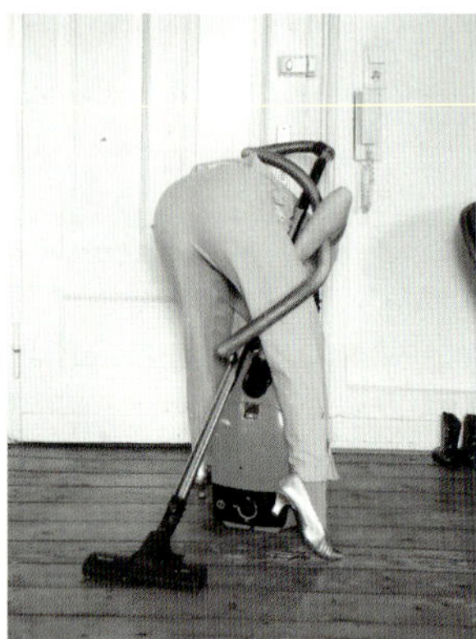
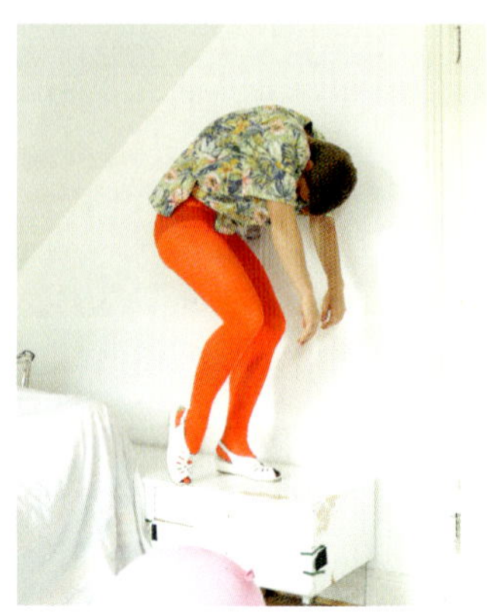
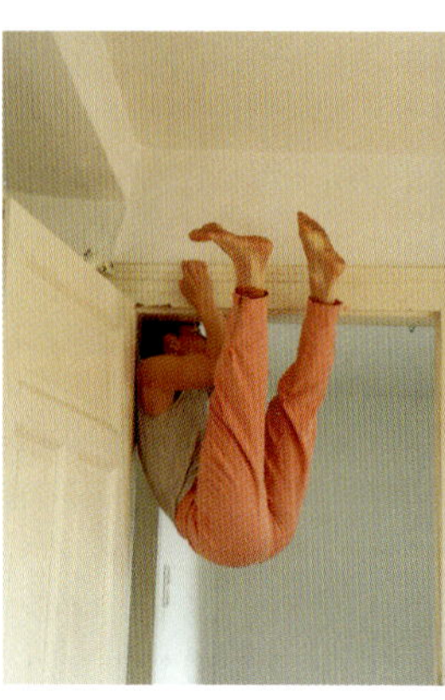

Top: *Garden 5*, 2020 and *Door 2.3*, 2021
Middle: *Schlafzimmer 8*, 2021 and *Staubsauger 1*, 2020
Bottom: *Home 22_1*, 2021 and *Door 2.3*, 2020

Did lockdown change your relationship with your body?

What is normally a seamless or uncomplicated relationship between architecture and the human body enters into a state of tense friction in Isabelle Wenzel's photographs titled Until Further Notice. In images taken during the periods of enforced isolation in response to the COVID-19 pandemic, Wenzel, a former acrobat, is shown twisting herself around tables, vacuum cleaners, and houseplants. She hangs from door frames, contorts herself into furniture, and does headstands in the corner. Some of her positions defy the laws of physics, having been frozen mid-fall by the momentary magic of photography; in others, she demonstrates great physical strength and endurance. Wenzel's face is often hidden or obscured, which shifts her photographs away from being about her or of her, and instead her body becomes a piece of sculpture to be explored and contorted for the camera. Trapped in a repetitive daily cycle in a small apartment, Wenzel uses her body as a means of expanding the space around her, disrupting the relationship between herself and the architecture and objects that have been ergonomically designed to accommodate the human form. Alone and using the camera's timer, Wenzel seems obsessive in her antics, perhaps even a little reckless during a time when self-protection was paramount. Rather than the body relenting to such a situation—to stay inside and to stay safe and still—it enters into a performative protest, albeit in private. Wenzel's body becomes a representation of her mental state while in lockdown, a state that so many of us shared: one of confinement, endless repetition, and pent-up energy.

Do you think of porn stars as people?

Her name is Mlle Mystere—at least that's the name we, her audience, know her by. I doubt this is her actual name; knowing that might add a layer of unappealing intimacy. As a webcam girl, she is, in the eyes of those who gaze upon her, nothing more than a female body, paid by the minute to satisfy the sexual desires of a mostly male audience. Yet here, the desires of her audience are not quite clear. Judging by her pose, which seems a touch traditional, perhaps she is performing for someone who derives more pleasure from art history than from watching women perform sexual acts online. For her series Cam Girls, Kate Peters sought out female webcammers who work from home. Often these women are juggling domestic responsibilities with the erotic demands of strangers. They are self-employed and acting under their own volition; their bodies are commodities, their means to make rent each month or to pay tuition fees, but they are also their bodies—bodies that cook dinner, clean the toilet, and perhaps rock the baby to sleep.

Through the screen, Peters directed these women, asking them to pose with props, adjust their staging, and tweak the lighting. She would then take screenshots which she rephoto-graphed with a medium-format camera. The visual clarity of such a camera crystallizes the poor quality of the Internet connection, so that we become actually aware of the state of separation created by the screen. This visual texture also creates a serenity, a sense of calm not usually associated with sex work. This soft, painterly effect, combined with the lighting and staging, calls to

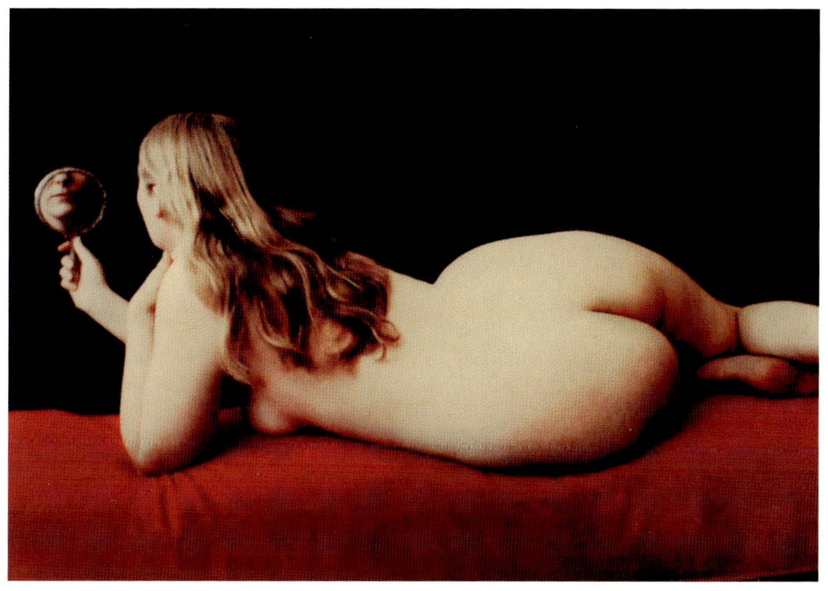

mind the women represented in historical paintings and in early photography, a medium to which pornography owes a great deal. Though one could argue that these women already hold power and authority as objects of desire, here that position is not fueled by the hypercharged expectations of the male gaze. The clear and convivial collaboration between Peters and her subjects disrupts the Internet's tendency to reduce the female body to an object of sexual fantasy, to be experienced remotely in order to satisfy the needs of others.

Above: *Mlle Mystere (Mirror)*, 2013 | Following spread: *Zareen (Recline)*, 2013

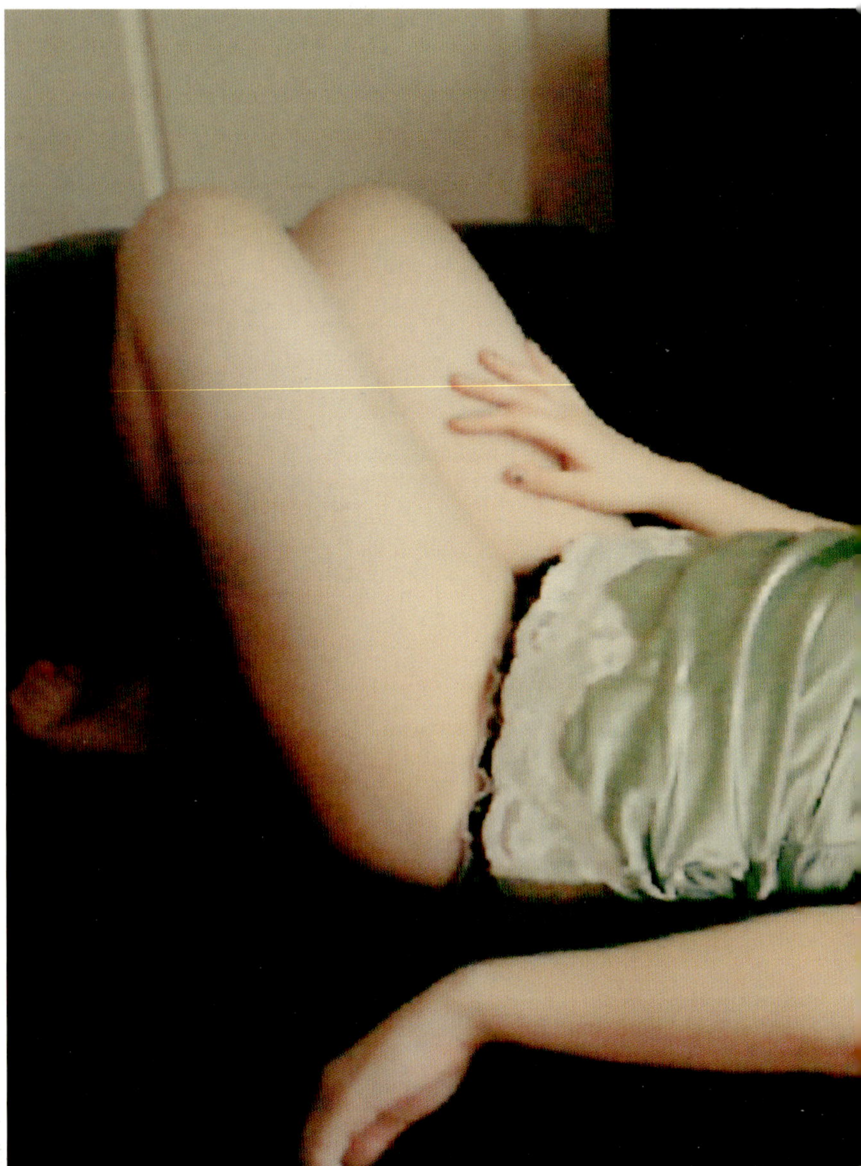

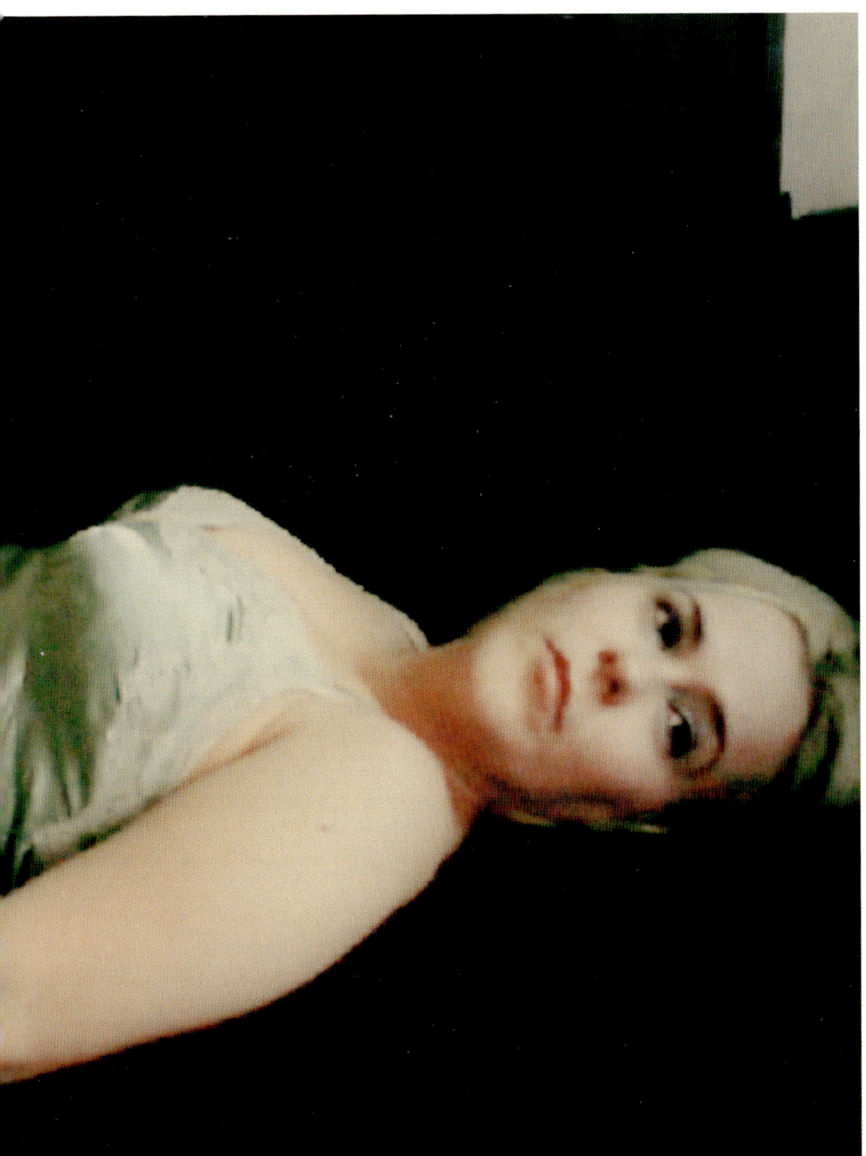

What is a human body supposed to look like?

She looks so glamorous, doesn't she, sitting there gazing off frame into the soft natural light, surrounded by ornate furnishings and adorned with stuffed tentacular limbs. But a startling realization takes place as we try to distinguish fabric from flesh. Apart from her right forearm and hand, as we travel down the image, her lower body becomes unrecognizable. Her left hand is a pincer and her right leg has no foot. At the age of nine, Mari Katayama chose to have her lower legs amputated after being born with tibial hemimelia. This rare developmental condition presented a profound yet pragmatic choice for someone so young; keep her legs and be bound to a wheelchair or give them up and be able to walk with the aid of prosthetics. Now Katayama's body plays an integral role in her process of creative self-expression. Stitching prosthetic limbs that incorporate shells, pearls, and crystals, Katayama makes elaborate costumes that push her body into increasing states of obscurity.

In some images, she is clearly trying to appear like a crustacean, a creature physically at odds with the human form. In others, she reclines on a bed of handmade furnishings and accessorized prosthetics, allowing us to see her unfamiliar body in its entirety. Always she appears stoic and proud, but a healthy dose of performative humor also creeps in. Katayama is a lady playing dress-up, and her elaborate costumes often make her appear like a sea creature, albeit a very chic, enigmatic one. Though we can read her work as attempting to shift our perceptions about what the human body should look like—make us a little more accepting of "deformity"—such a reading does, in itself, form a barrier to acceptance, to physical inclusivity. Katayama is an artist like any other. All she wants is for us to relish the immersive beauty of her creations.

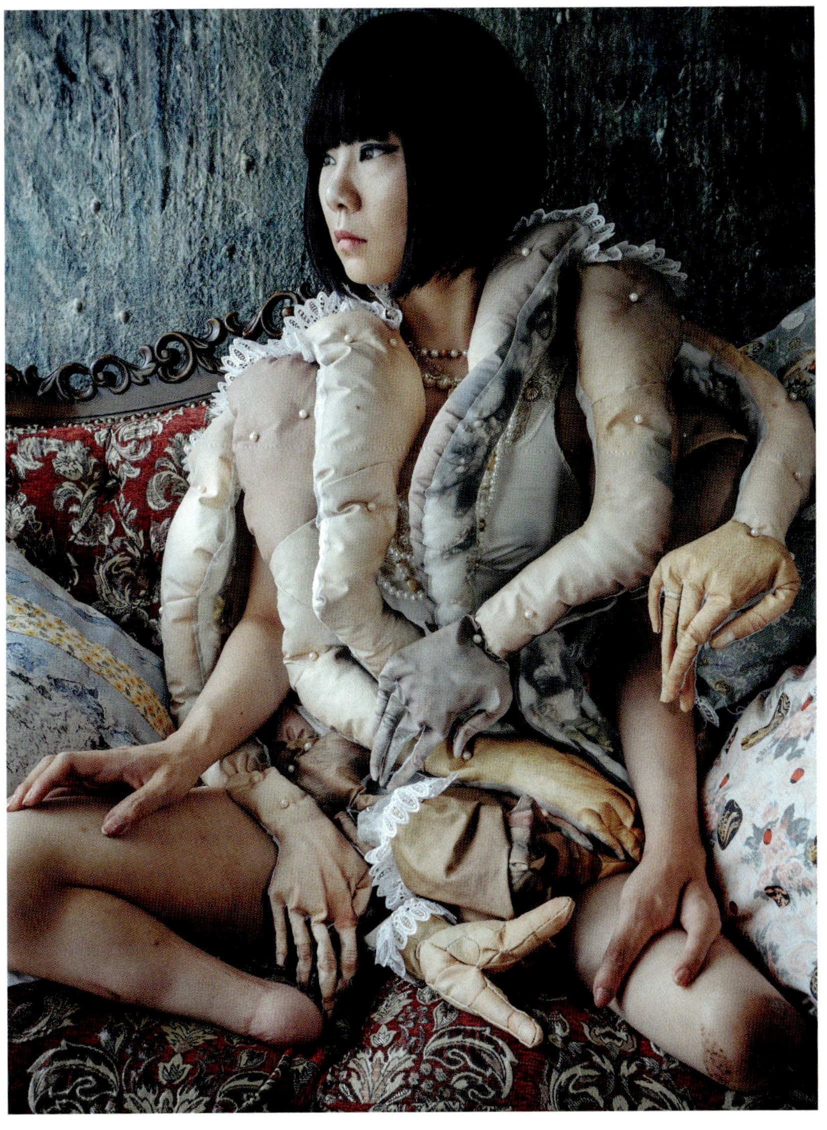

Above: *Bystander #023*, 2016 | Following spread: *Bystander #022*, 2016

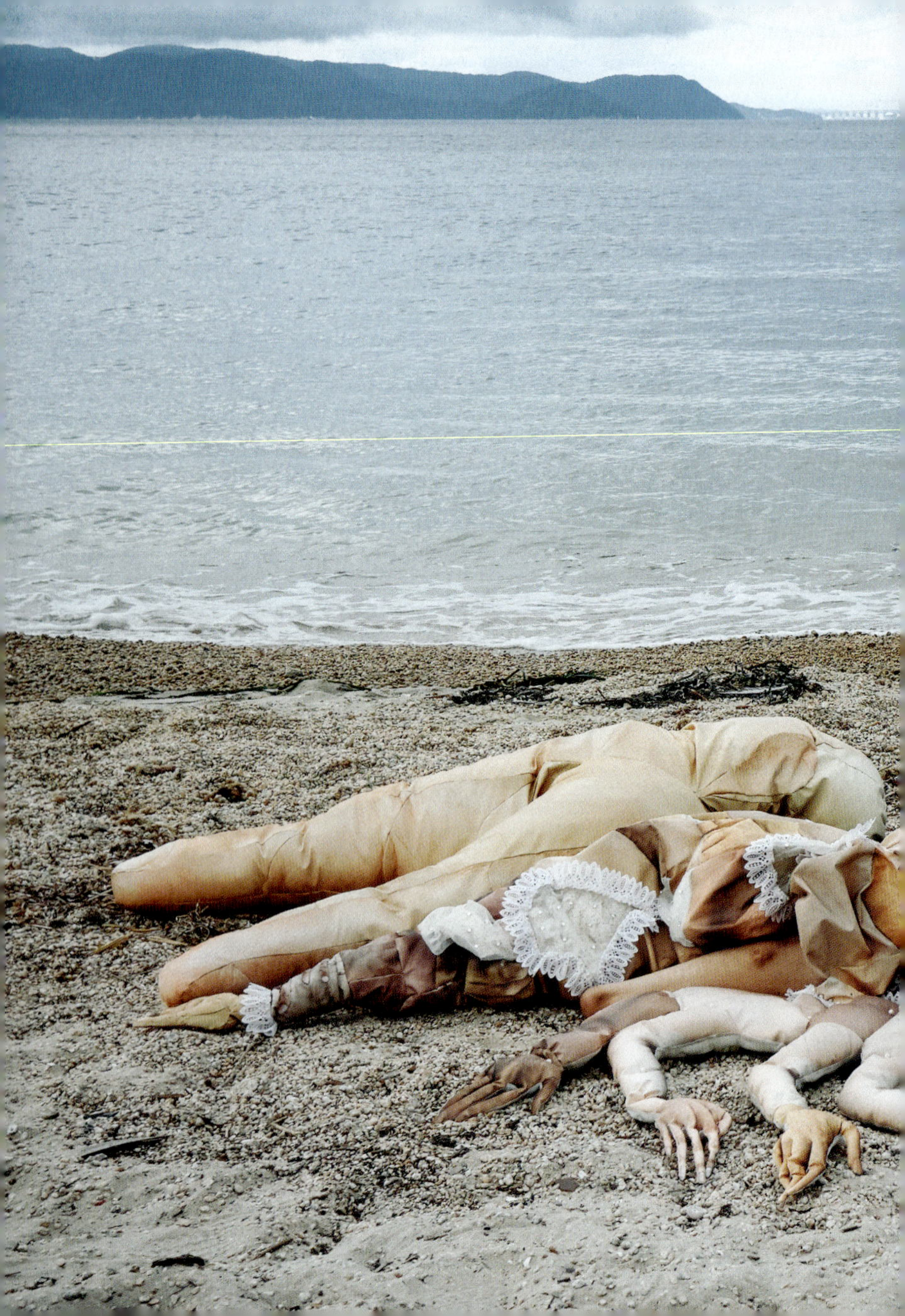

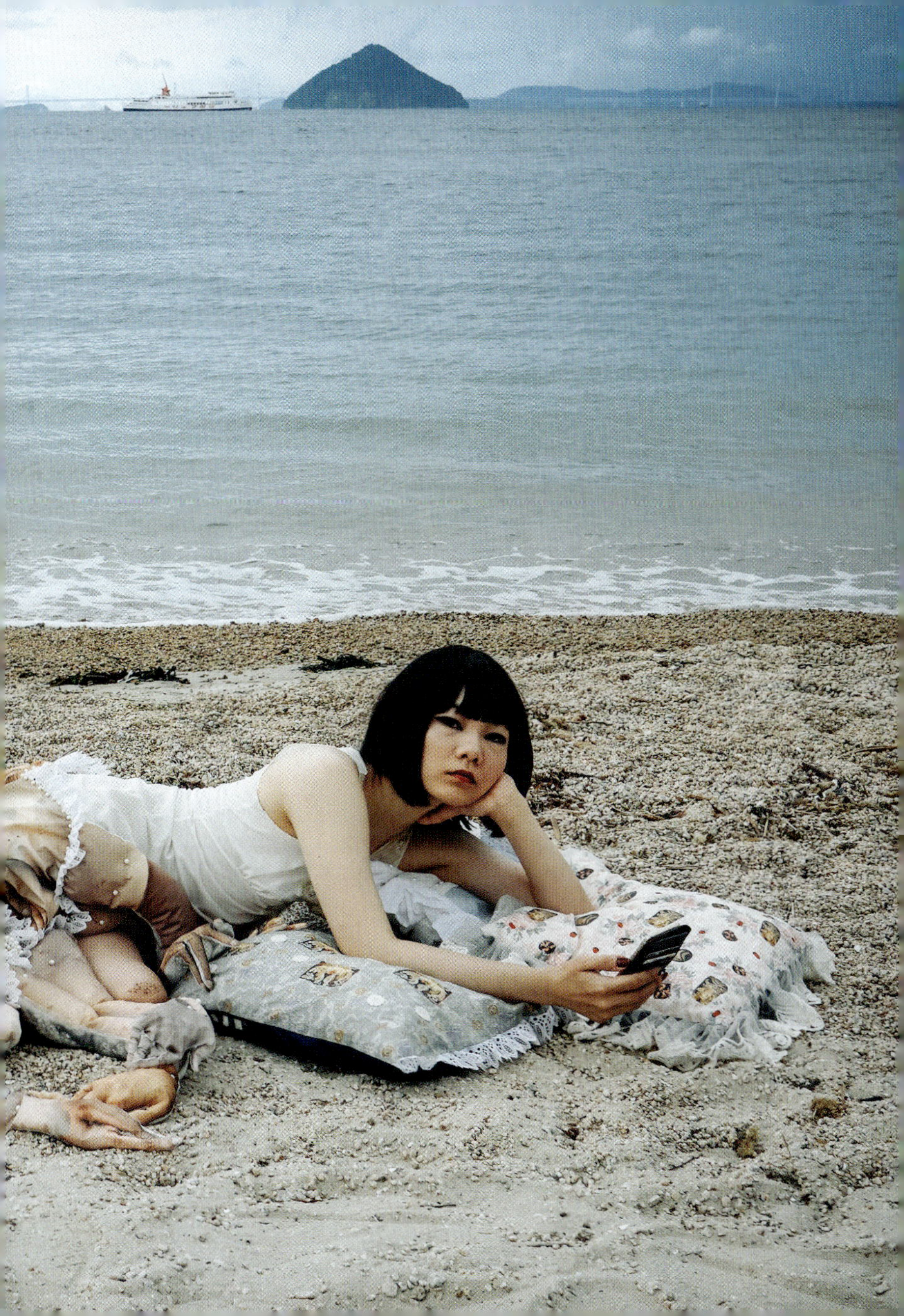

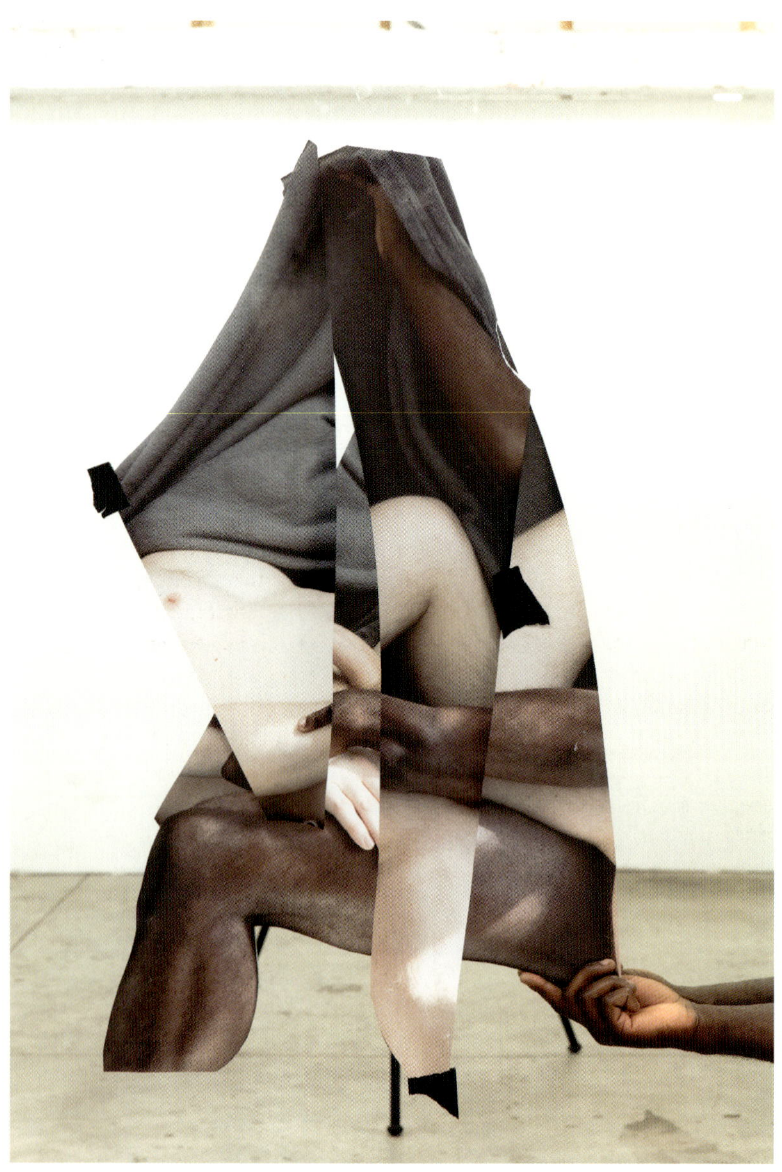

Mirror Study (0X5A6571), 2018

Do you have a private and a public gaze?

If it wasn't for the fact that one body is dark and the other so pale, it would be impossible to make sense of this dissected arrangement of limbs in Paul Mpagi Sepuya's photograph. From this initial point of clarity, a kind of domino effect occurs that collapses the other layers of construction and deconstruction. The two interwoven bodies form a collage that appears to be taped to thin air; behind this assembly, the studio is on full show. No attempt has been made to hide it, which, for some, might be more startling than the entanglement of homoerotic desire in the foreground. Then there are the legs of a tripod on which the camera must be mounted; essentially the source of our gaze. But how can we be both in front of and behind the subject? It is the reflected arm of the photographer that reveals the use of a mirror. The background is a reflection onto which the bodies are placed. What might have initially appeared haphazard is, in fact, meticulous. In making visible the mechanisms of photography and by involving friends and lovers as models, Sepuya redefines the studio as a playful, social space where one can openly explore one's sexuality. Within this informal and collaborative process, a very honest form of self-expression reveals itself, one that is not solely reliant on the photographer looking and controlling the subject. Ultimately, Sepuya's images become self-referential explorations addressing a gap in photographic representation that has traditionally excluded the queer gaze of photographers of color.

With Cuts: A Traditional Sculpture, the trans artist Cassils commits to a physically and psychologically obsessive performance, documenting a twenty-three-week course of body-building. Inspired by Eleanor Antin's 1972 performance, *Carving: A Traditional Sculpture*, for which the artist crash-dieted for forty-five days, Cassils sets out to reverse the process by gaining twenty-three pounds of muscle by means of a protein-rich diet, steroids, and rigorous workouts. Photographing their transforming body throughout the process, Cassils presents the resulting images in grids. The images show no evidence of the grueling psychological effects of this process—only the physical. As such, they force us to contemplate Cassils's body as an image. Our conditioning through previous representations of the body, which have been very binary, prompt us to find a label of either male or female. But that is not possible here; human biology and social constructs collide, and neither one wins over. Perhaps some might consider the results of Cassils's reimagining of the body as a kind of Venn diagram, in which the artist sits in the middle. But that, too, would be an understanding of the human body in terms of male or female. By occupying a previously unrepresented domain in visual culture, Cassils suggests a need for new parameters with which to consider and appreciate the human form.

Why is the first question we ask expecting parents, "Is it a boy or a girl?"

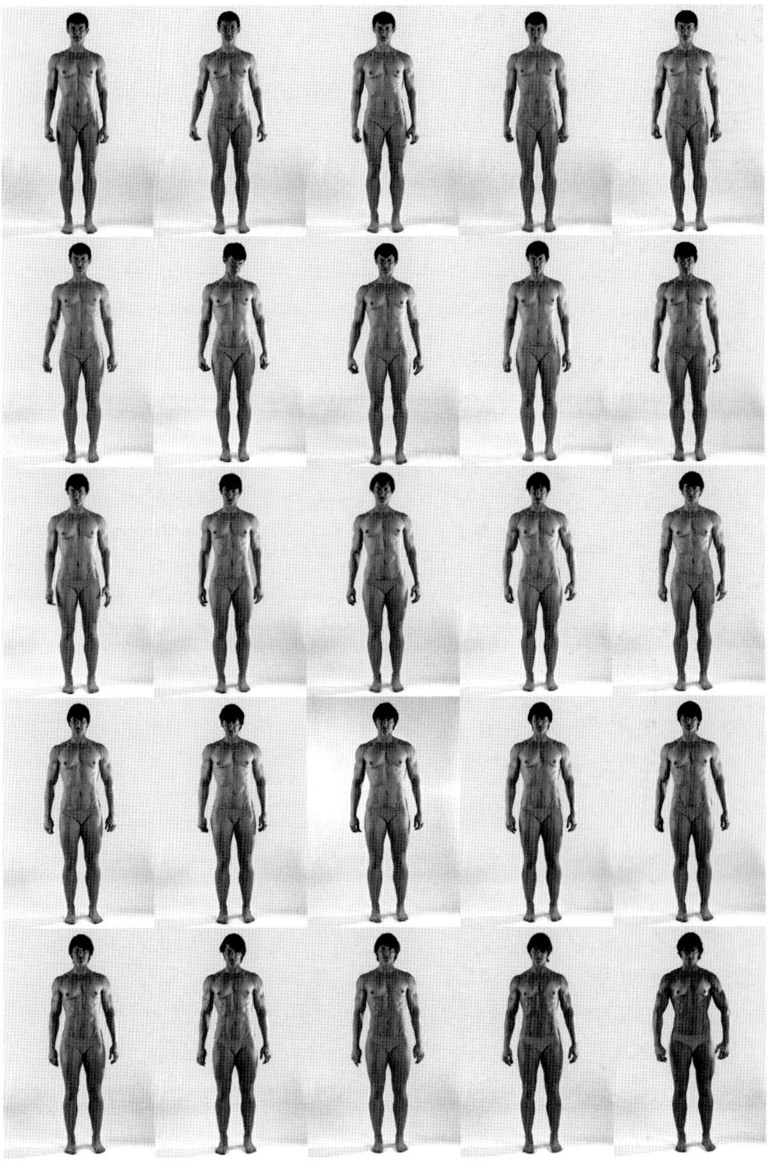

Time Lapse (Front), from Cuts: A Traditional Sculpture, 2011

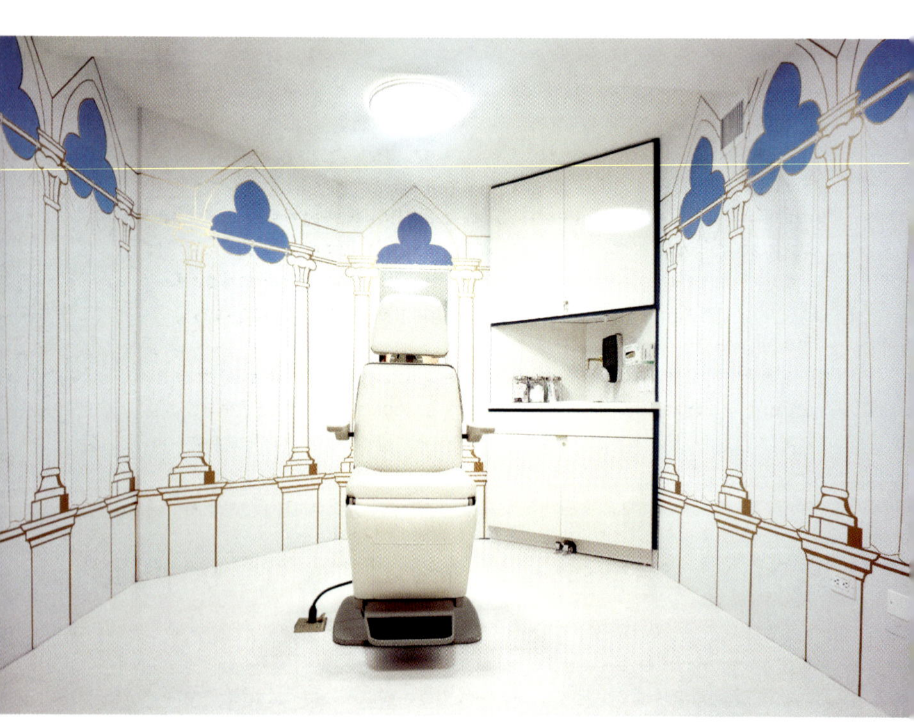

White Consultation Room, Upper East Side, New York, NY, 2006

Is cosmetic surgery a form of self-harm?

In a culture that expects us to be attractive, we find that the standards of beauty are being pushed to the extreme. A former child model and makeup-counter clerk, Cara Phillips is all too familiar with the psychological burdens that grow out of this cause-and-effect cycle of chasing beauty. Her photographs—taken inside the offices of cosmetic surgeons—depict consultation chairs, machines on wheels, "Botox mood charts," and examples of successfully enhanced body parts to choose from. Stark and utterly lacking in warmth, these rooms purport to offer a cure for an illness they are, in fact, perpetuating: physical inadequacy and insecurity.

Here, without the presence of a doctor or patient, we are left to scrutinize the room itself, trying to locate any imperfections that will make the space feel a little more human. Yet there are none. Everything appears pristine, no dust or scuffs on a flawless white floor. Even the Romanesque design flourish on the walls seems to add to the sterility and enhance the feeling of artifice. And look at that ceiling light. It glows like a halo above an empty chair, as if waiting to crown the soon-to-be-perfect being who sits beneath it. With this empty room, Phillips finds an apt metaphor that speaks to the culture of cosmetic surgery, of those in search of a flawless facade that does not necessarily need to look or feel natural.

Whatever motivates someone to go under the knife is, of course, a deeply personal matter. That said, cosmetic procedures are just that—cosmetic. They alter one's physical appearance, not one's genes. With that in mind, I wonder what cosmetically altered couples must think of their biological newborns? Their child would, I suppose, confront them with their natural self, what they regard as their imperfect self.

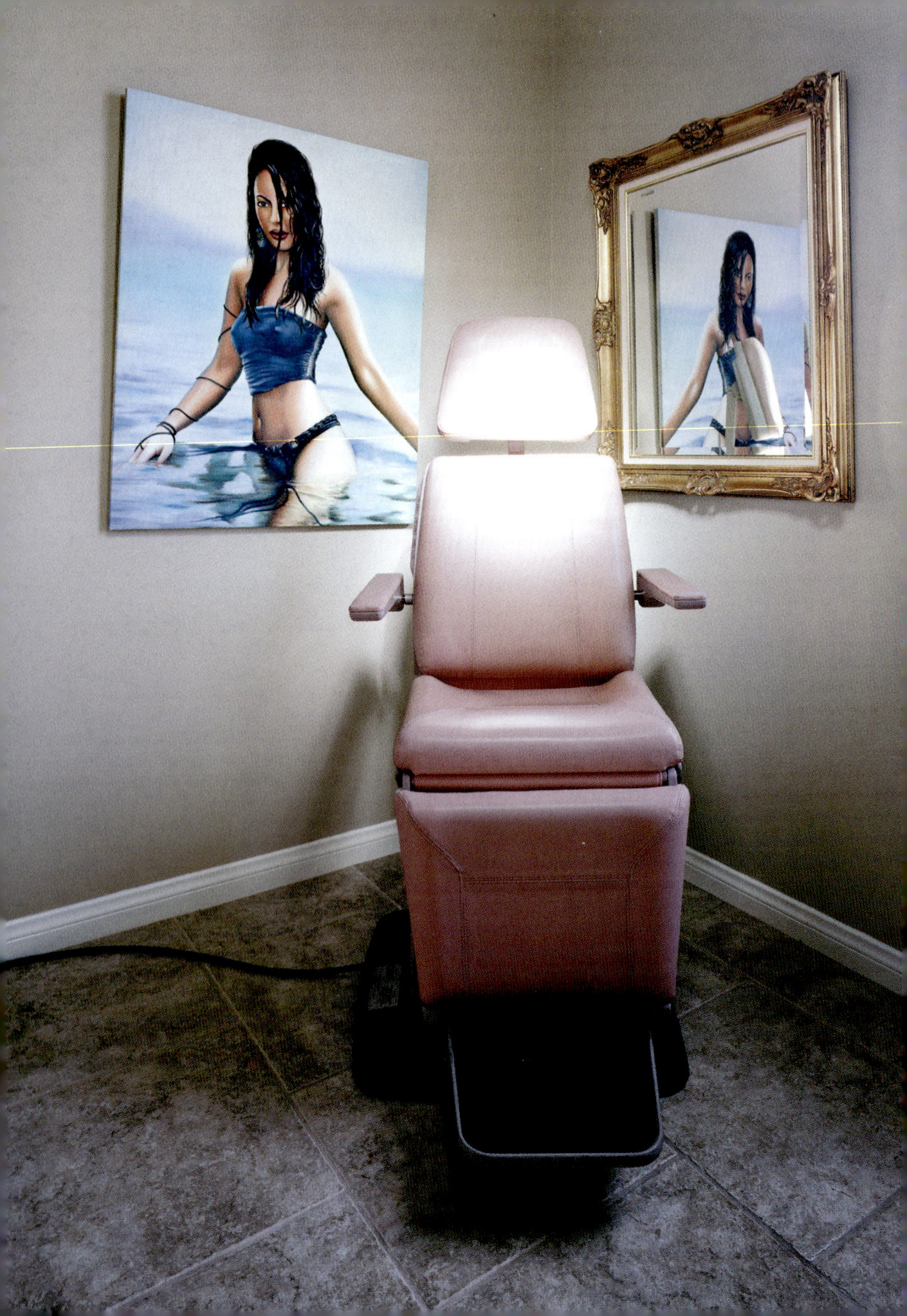

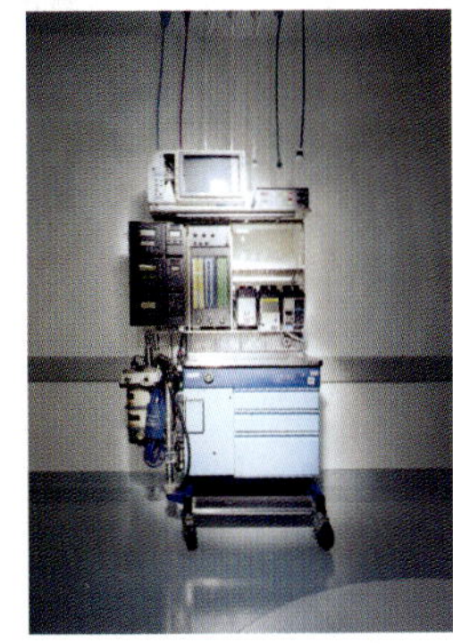

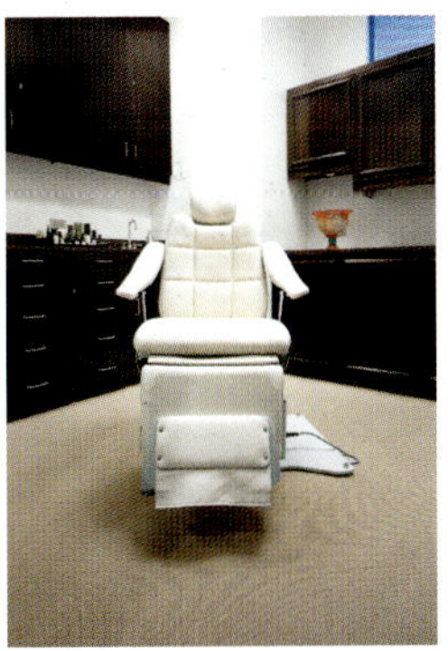

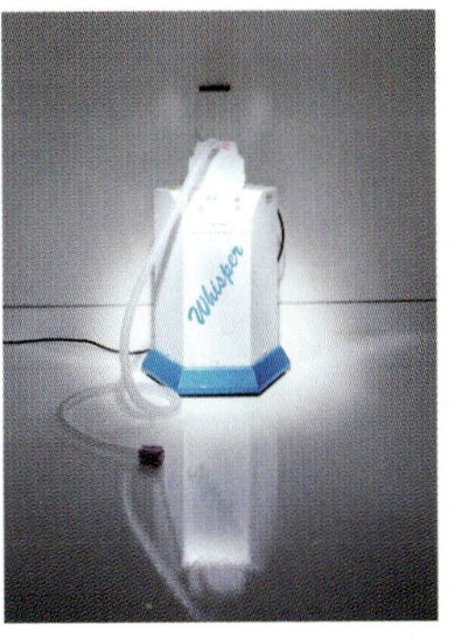

Opposite: *Playboy Consultation Chair, Orange County, CA, 2007*
Above (top to bottom): *Blue Anesthesia Machine, Century City, Los Angeles, CA, 2007*
Beige Consultation Chair, Beverly Hills, CA, 2007
The Whisper, Washington, D.C., 2008

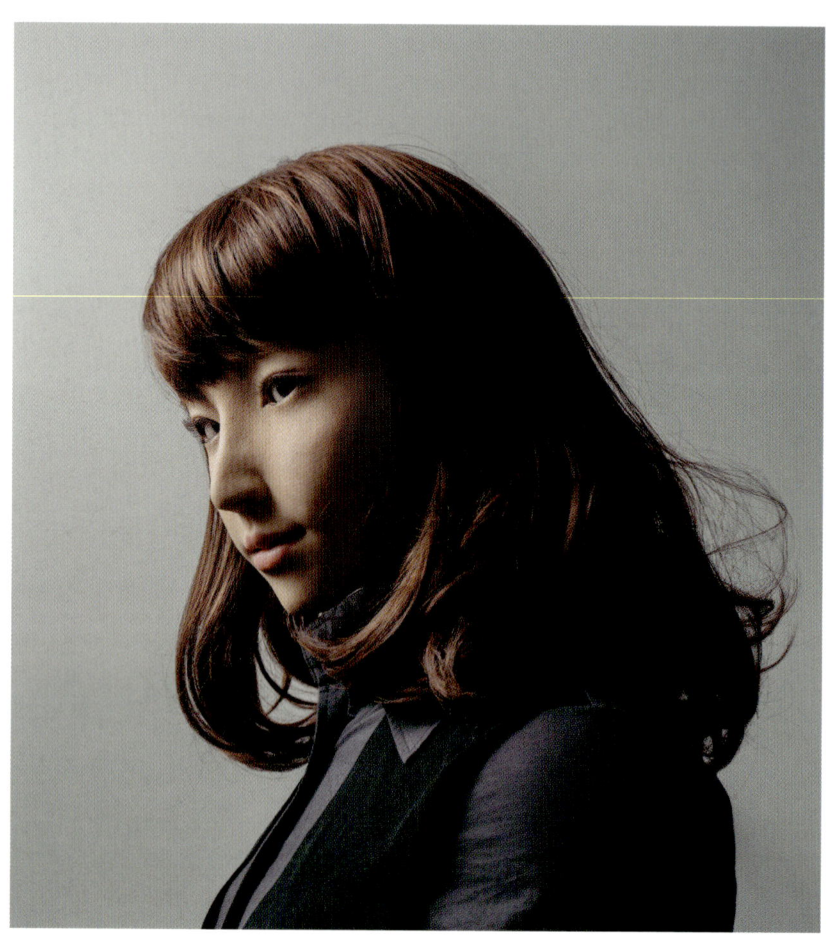

Above and following spread: *One of Them Is a Human, #1–3*, 2017

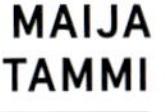

Will androids be content with their bodies?

Maija Tammi's series starts out as a playful game, one that instantly engages us with its title: One of Them Is a Human. Yet as we start to analyze expressions, skin, and hair, each subject has the potential to be a real human, and each has the potential to be something else, in this case, a state-of-the-art android. The position of uncertainty in which we find ourselves calls into question the set of criteria we apply when deciding what humans, and androids, should look like. One understanding is innate—humans know humans—whereas the other has been shaped by science fiction and the possibilities of technology. But as androids become more advanced, more "lifelike," and medical procedures and beauty trends push humans to be more "artificial," how will this affect our understanding of our bodies and an android's understanding of its body?

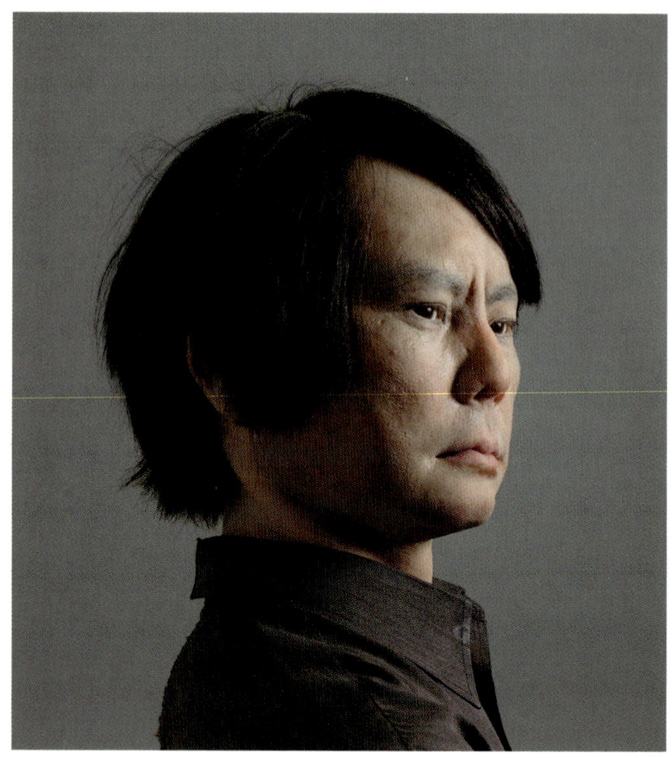

By photographing these androids alongside a real human, Tammi confronts us with representations of representations, a process that disrupts, or preempts, our innate tendency to distinguish between what is living and what is not. Early photography prompted reactions ranging from shock to confusion and ambivalence at seeing someone so lifelike but lifeless, and perhaps the same will be true for our acceptance of androids. As in the case of photography, we will become so accustomed to seeing ourselves mirrored by technology that this will further

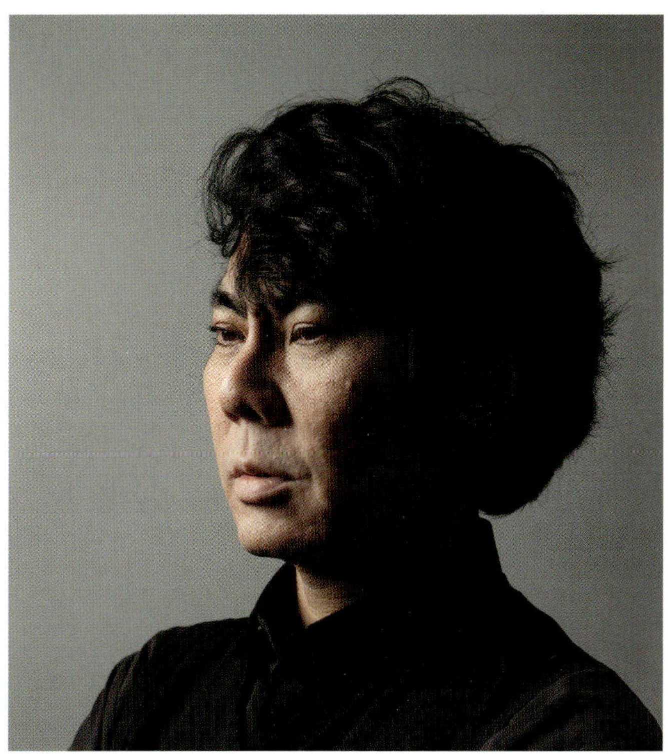

shape how we perceive ourselves. Perhaps we might increasingly aspire to look more like them, rather than want them to look more like us. But what will happen in a slightly more distant future if and when androids design themselves? Will they feel any emotional or physical tie to their human forms, or will they simply redesign their bodies without any concern for the fact that they were created by us, in our own image? And, in any case, what will our image be at that point?

FAITH

Years ago, my friend Ahmed helped me lead photography tours in Morocco. Ahmed was on hand to assist guests with whatever they needed, but during tours he would occasionally disappear for a few moments, often when everyone sat down to lunch at the riad or presented their pictures on the roof terrace. "Where's Ahmed?" guests would impatiently demand when filled with the sudden urge to buy a silver teapot or leather pouf. They would always forget he was praying. Ahmed's prayer breaks became as routine for me as they were for him, so much so that I abruptly walked in on him crouched on the floor, or standing bolt upright, chanting words I did not understand. The mundane spaces he co-opted—laundry rooms, spas, pantries— would, for five or so minutes, become filled with an invisible fog of reverence. He would be so immersed in, almost possessed by, prayer that he never once reacted to or even noticed my intrusion. Yet it was unsettling to see Ahmed, someone normally so attentive, so aware of others, in a state of being there but not there. Inevitably, I would tiptoe out, embarrassed, intimidated even, as if I had witnessed something not meant for me, something above my spiritual pay grade. But what exactly had I witnessed? My reaction seemed triggered not by what I could see but by what I couldn't: Ahmed's faith, something immense and powerful that almost turned the air tactile at times yet remained invisible—to me, at least.

This "presence in absence" makes faith an intriguing and challenging subject for photography. How does one photograph what one cannot see? How does one find significance in something that means everything to one person and nothing to the next? Photography is, after all, very specific in that it requires a subject that can be seen, a fact. Yet photographs are inherently ambiguous and open to interpretation: They are fictions. Image makers, however, find themselves in the privileged position of being able to explore—a word they love—without needing to come up with definite answers or prove anything at all. Perhaps, then, photography is in fact an excellent medium through which to encounter and reflect on a subject both enigmatic and omnipresent. Religious or spiritual faith does, after all, play a part in all our lives. It impacts social structures, influences laws, and shapes the moral codes by which we live. It also satisfies another distinctly human need: to believe in, or belong to, something far greater than ourselves. Faith in sports teams, political parties, nations, and even art helps us to find meaning, purpose, and a sense of identity during our infinitesimally short time on Earth. It also helps us come to terms with the biggie, the one certainty in life, which is death.

The following work draws on deeply personal experiences in order to grapple with a uniquely human characteristic. The photographers are neither trying to convince us to believe nor ridiculing those who do. Their intentions are simply to provoke thought and reflection on an aspect of humanity that—whether or not you are a believer—touches us all.

How does one
photograph
what one
cannot see?

**ANA
ZIBELNIK**

What are the positives of death?

Here, American Sign Language is captured by Ana Zibelnik in another silent language—that of photography. And the gesture pictured (one palm down, the other up) signifies something we must all come to terms with, in our own ways: It is the sign for death. The "possibility of impossibility" is how the philosopher Martin Heidegger described what lies at the heart of our preoccupation with death. He proposed that an acceptance of death, and of the nothingness that might await us all, heightens our sense of being alive: in essence, that we cannot live without dying. Zibelnik uses photography—a medium with close ties to the past, to moments gone, to traces of what once was—to reflect on the human awareness of mortality. Images of hands turning are situated beside desolated, wooded landscapes and repeated portraits of a young girl. An elderly couple has their backs to the camera, and a gloved hand holds the carcass of a butterfly. While Heidegger's philosophy might seem a little morbid, it is, in fact, quite upbeat. Zibelnik, too, draws on the paradoxical notion of the "possibility of impossibility" to piece together a narrative that finds solace somewhere other than religion or science. Rather, her photographs feel like moments of heightened awareness, a state that Heidegger described simply as "being."

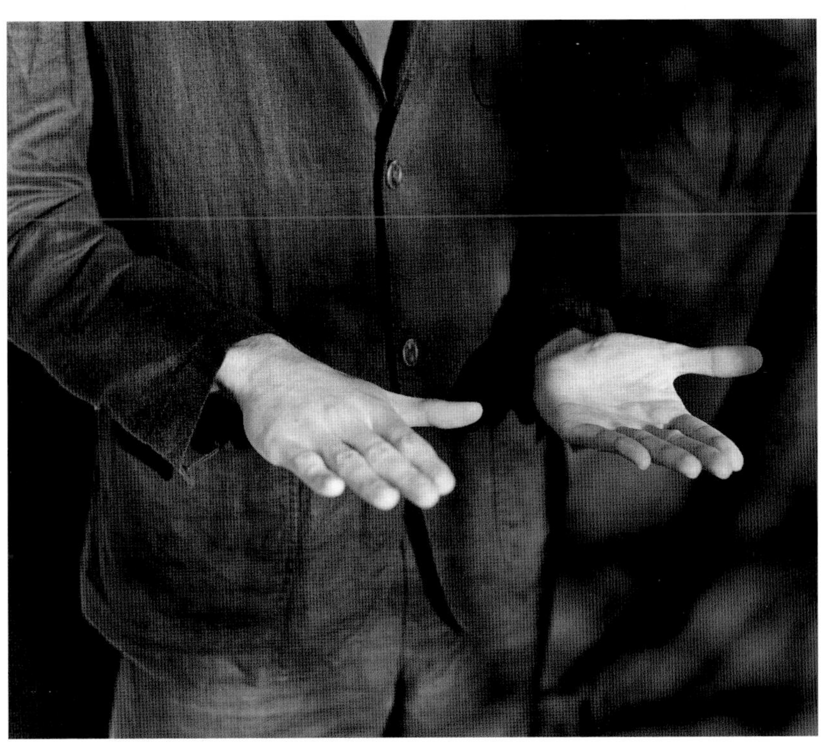

Above and following spread: Photos from the series We Are the Ones Turning, 2019

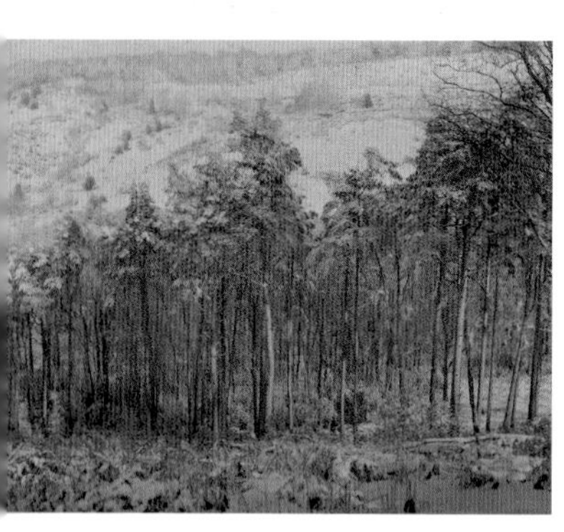

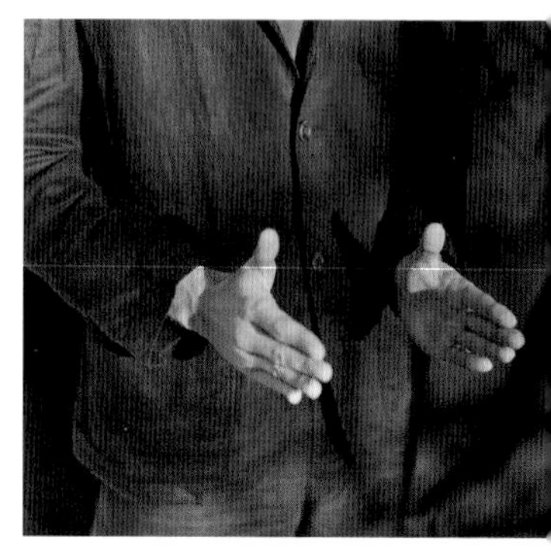

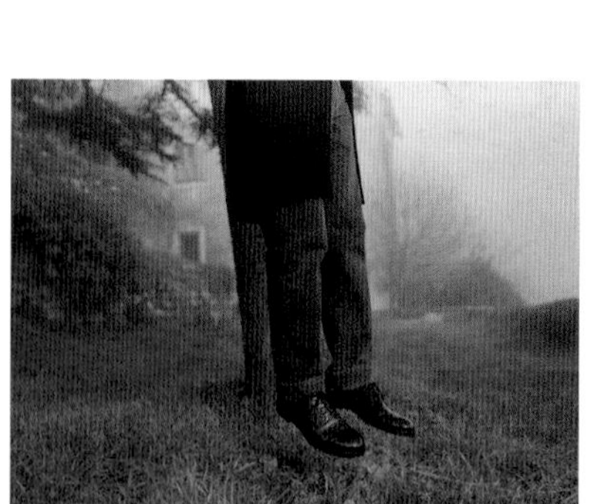

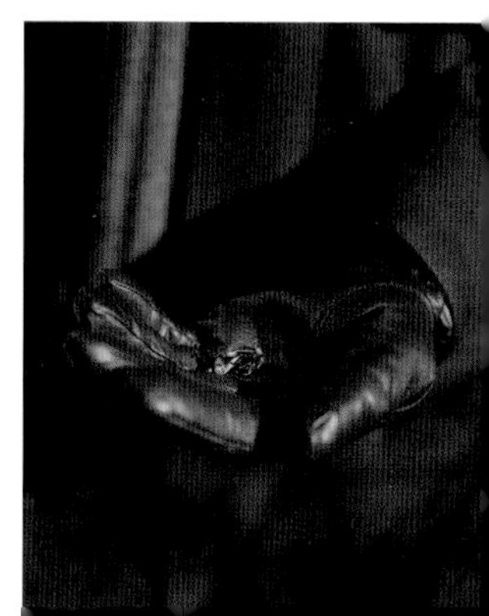

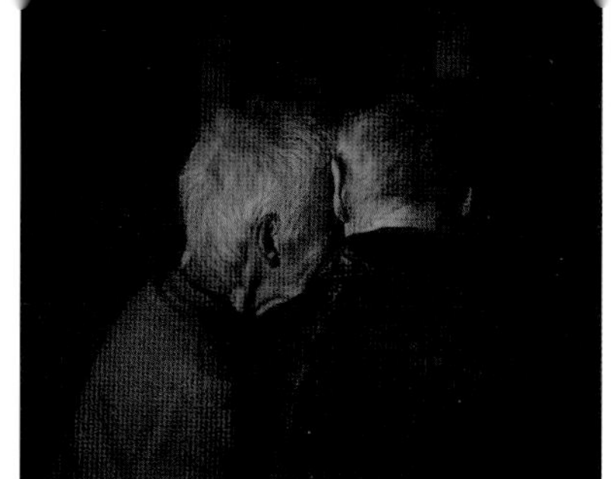

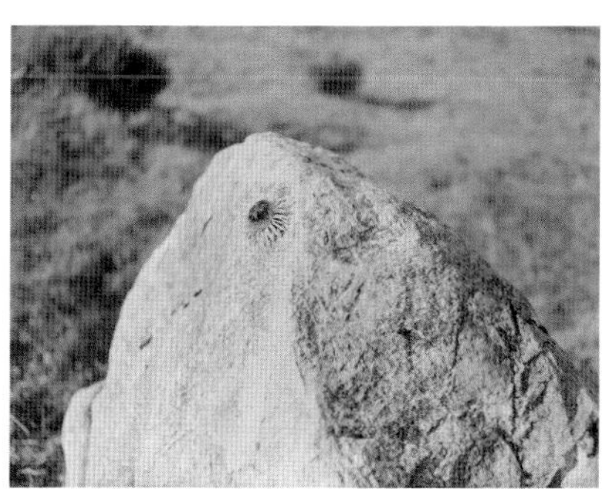

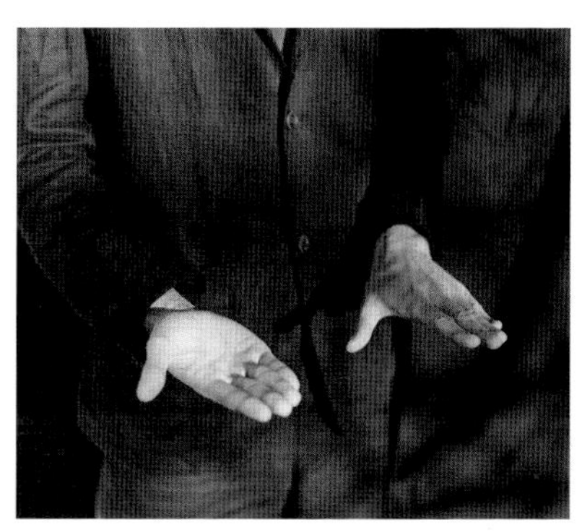

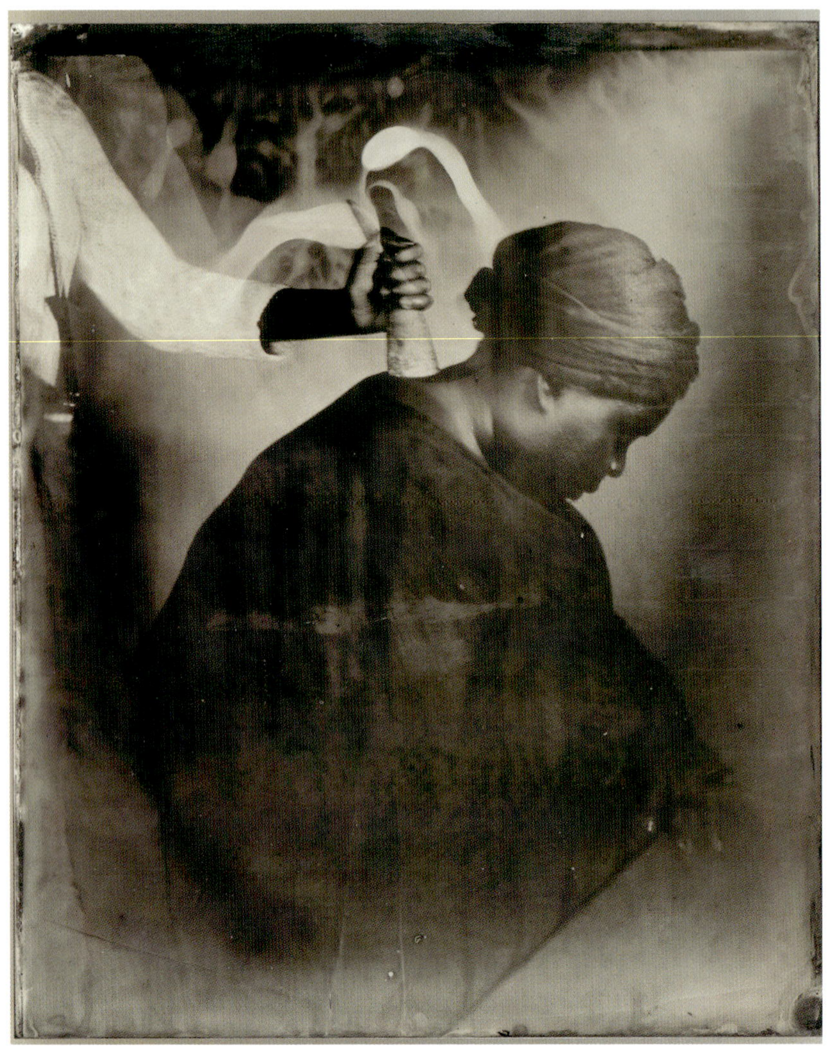

Nak Bejjen, 2017

Can photography picture the unseen?

Dressed in a dark gown, the subject's body appears to emerge from the depths of the image, her head bowed in prayer; an object is being pressed against the nape of her neck. But something else, something less tangible, is also present in the image: a smokiness. And what looks to be watermarks of varying exposures infuse this moment like manifestations of ectoplasm.

Photography itself becomes part of the spiritual healing process for Khadija Saye. Saye turned to traditional spiritual practices of West Africa to heal traumas of the past and seek mental and physical grounding. In this self-portrait, we see Saye taking part in a traditional Gambian ritual involving a sacred cow horn. The work is a one-off, being a collodion tintype, in which a metal plate is dipped in a light-sensitive silver nitrate solution and exposed when wet—an almost baptismal photographic process, one of slow and delicate submersion and cleansing in order to achieve an image. The plate is then developed and the image fixed before it has a chance to dry. The wet emulsion can never be fully controlled, making it a process where the outcome is hard to predict. The knowledge and precision of the photographer ultimately comes down to an act of faith, a surrendering to the unknown magic of their medium.

Photography has evolved from something requiring patience and faith into something instantaneous and ubiquitous. Images once remained in a latent state on unexposed rolls of film for days, weeks, or months: there, yet not there. Now images reveal themselves at the moment of their creation; they make themselves known without any mystery and multiply exponentially. By deferring to traditional processes to embody ancient rituals, Saye multiplies the enigma of faith by the enigma of photography. Each of these tintypes is different, each special in its own way. They are precious keepsakes that speak to the intensely personal nature of faith.

**DAVID
AVAZZADEH**

Smartphones enhance our connection with others and the world around us. At least, that's how they're marketed. Hardly surprising, then, that these devices have become the perfect vehicle for peddling spirituality, which has become a convenient yet highly commodified means of connecting with ourselves. I (Falsely) Believe I Have This Thing Figured Out When I Really Haven't presents a series of locked iPhone screens created by David Avazzadeh, which he released one by one over the course of a year while recovering from a deep depression. In some assemblages, a familiar-sounding phrase coupled with a recently taken snapshot conforms to the trite visual language of online spirituality; "Leave room for others to grow" is placed over a picture of a houseplant dappled with sunlight. Others present a more amusing disconnect: "Let go of important parts of yourself to move on" appears over a snapshot of a human orifice. Familiar elements of the device's interface start to take on unintended relevance. The signal strength and power bar, for example, become tongue-in-cheek references to Avazzadeh's fluctuating mindset at very specific points in time. When combined with the interface of the iPhone, these phrases and images edge even further away from sincerity, from stirring any meaningful change or sense of empowerment, which is exactly how Avazzadeh apparently felt when he turned to them for answers. In his images, the notion of unlocking your phone becomes a humorous "swipe" at our superficial digital attempts to unlock ourselves.

Does your smartphone want you to be happy?

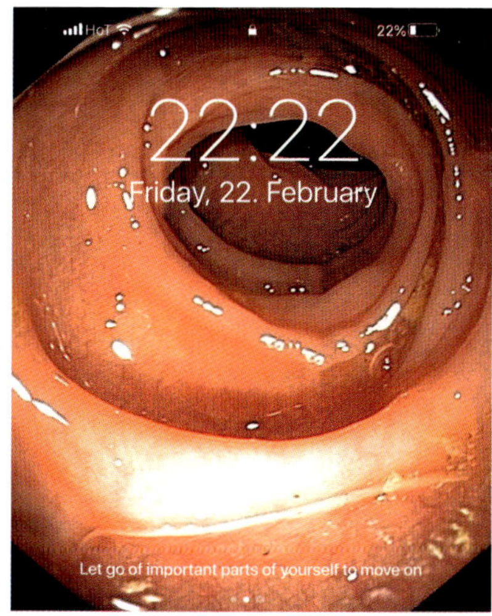

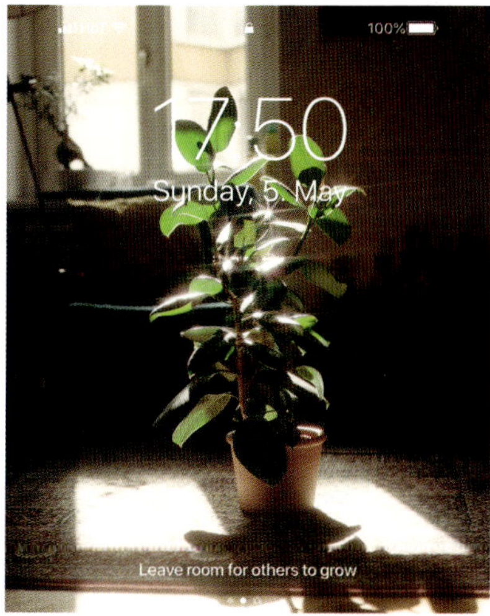

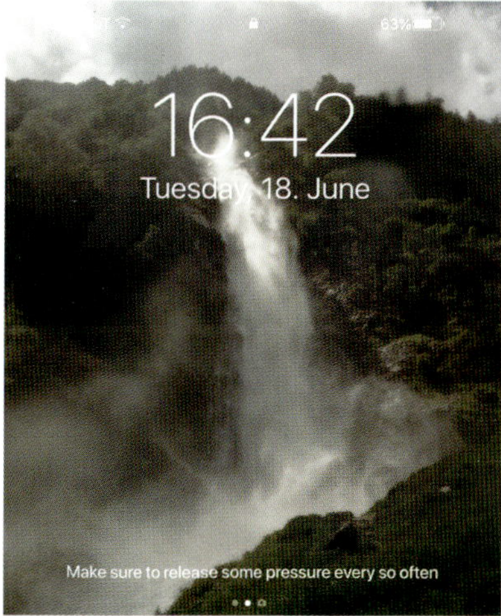

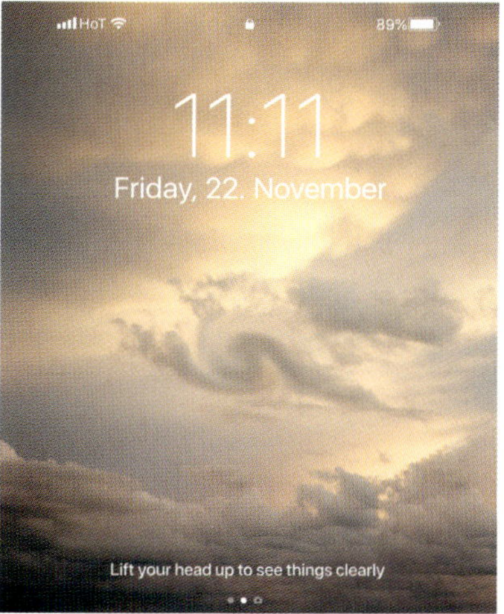

Clockwise from top left: *I (Falsely) Believe to Let Go*, 2019; *I (Falsely) Believe to Leave Room*, 2019; *I (Falsely) Believe to Lift Up*, 2019; *I (Falsely) Believe to Make Sure*, 2019

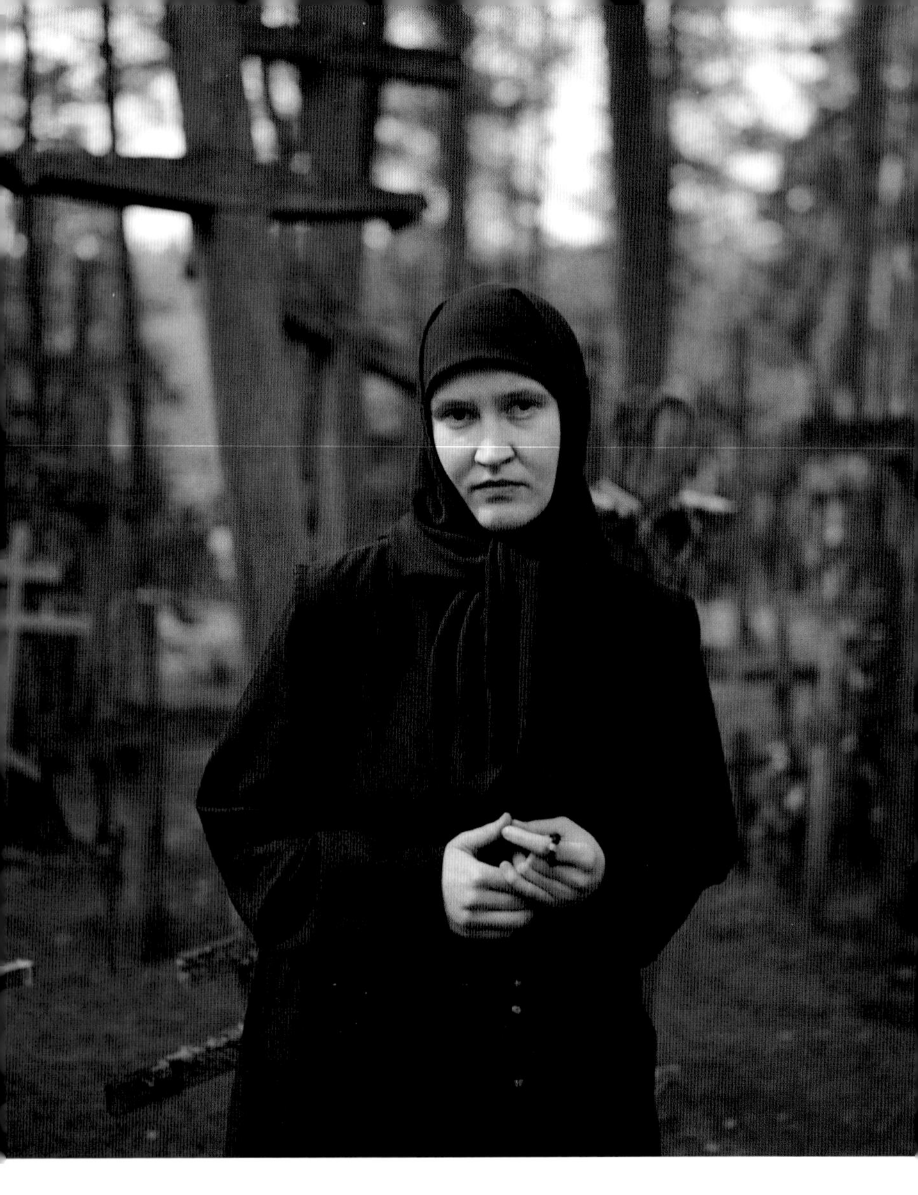

Above and following spread: Untitled, from the series Ex-Voto (2016–18)

Is it possible to share someone's faith?

Pilgrimage serves as a physical demonstration of faith in almost all religions: Muslims journey to Mecca for Hajj, Hindus to the Golden Temple located in the Holy City of Amritsar, Buddhists to sacred sites across Asia. With her series *Ex-Voto*, Alys Tomlinson documents Christian pilgrimages across Ireland, Poland, and France. Her tonally rich photographs of landscapes, pilgrims, and the offerings of thanks (or "ex-votos") they leave behind provide a glimpse of the invisible cord that ties together Heaven, humans, and Earth. In contrast to the jewel-encrusted image sometimes associated with Christianity, the ex-votos placed between rocks or etched on stone are handwritten and humble. The simplicity of the gesture that comes at the end of a long journey illustrates a purity of faith that sits outside the complexities and controversies of particular religions. At first the poses of the nameless people might seem guarded or hard to read, and the landscapes a little murky or sinister, but perhaps that is an instinctive response to seeing something that cannot be fully understood. After all, the practice of worship and the sacrifices one makes for faith are acts that truly make sense only to the individual. Tomlinson offers us images that are beautiful and ambiguous, comforting and unsettling. They are, themselves, ex-votos that suggest a person's faith is not something that needs to be explained.

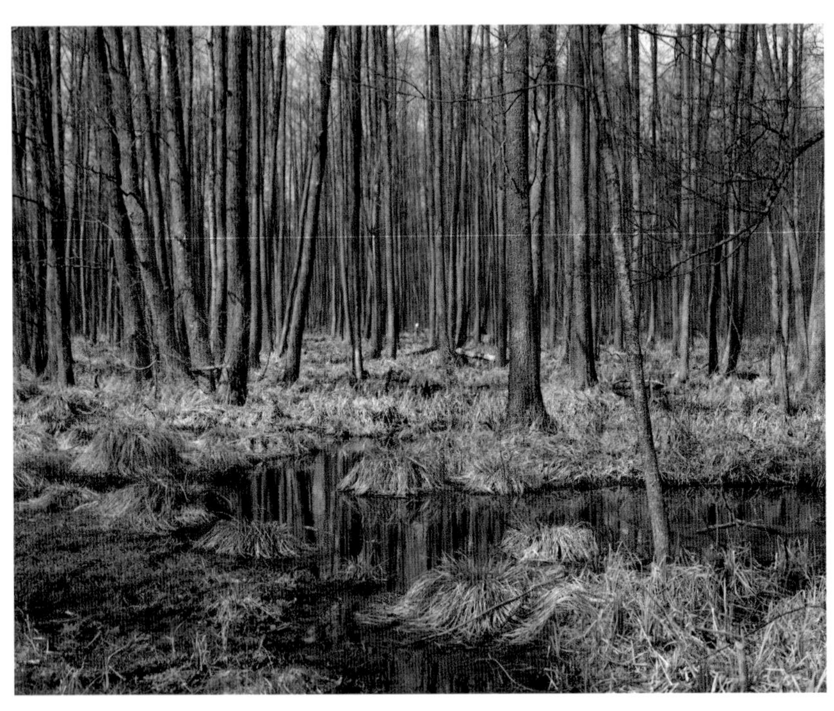

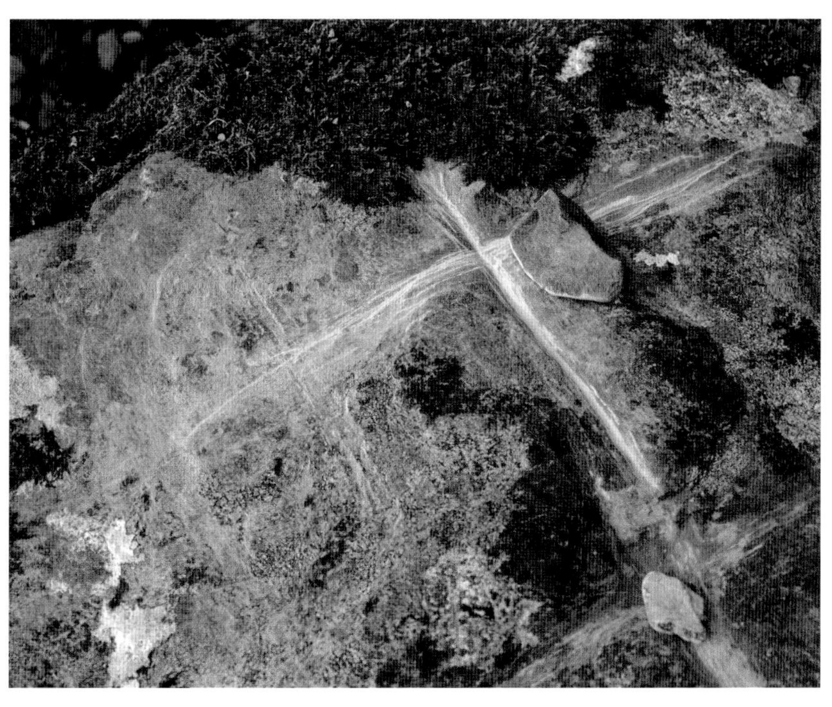

**PAWEL
JASZCZUK**

Can a mass-produced object be sacred?

With ¥€U, Pawel Jaszczuk turns our attention to the capitalism of Christianity. Using flash and a snapshot aesthetic, Jaszczuk's images depict Jesus on underwear and bath mats, as a glow-in-the-dark spaceman, and on the soles of shoes. These incarnations of Christ could be seen as disrespectful, as exposing the absurdity or irrelevance of religion and the kitsch, tasteless iconography that has developed around it. Yet one could read the global proliferation of such mass-produced religious products as a modern manifestation of Christian faith, a sign of its enduring appeal and importance. Many such products, no matter how tasteless and machine-made, serve as comforting keepsakes for believers to purchase at the gates of the Vatican or at the feet of Christ the Redeemer. And even the most blasphemous trinkets have their reverential side. A pair of Virgin Mary underwear, for example, might cross the line into intentional disrespect, but what is that disrespect if not a reaction, however childish, to the power of her image? Whether Christ appears above an altar or hangs from a rearview mirror, with ¥€U, Jaszczuk makes one thing perfectly clear: When it comes to making money, Christ is everywhere.

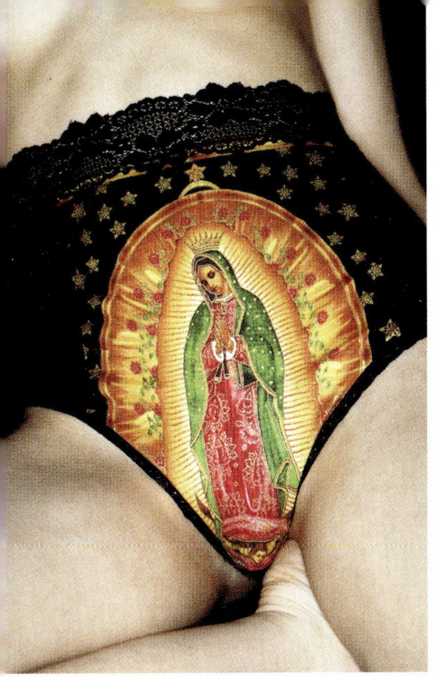

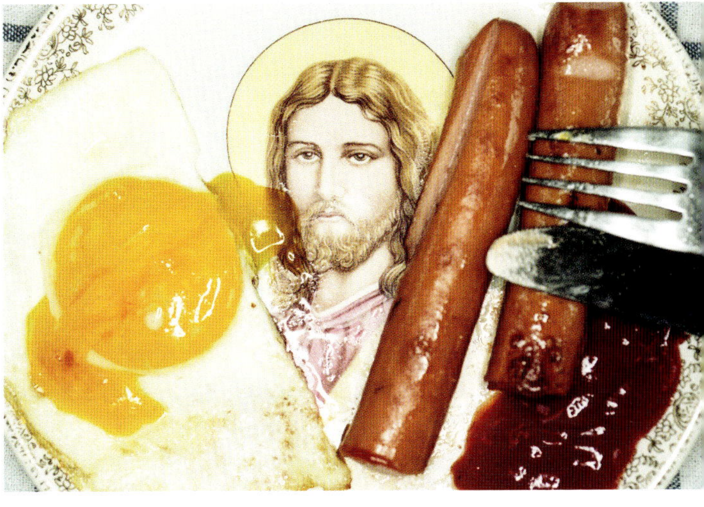

Above: Photos from the series ¥€U, 2018

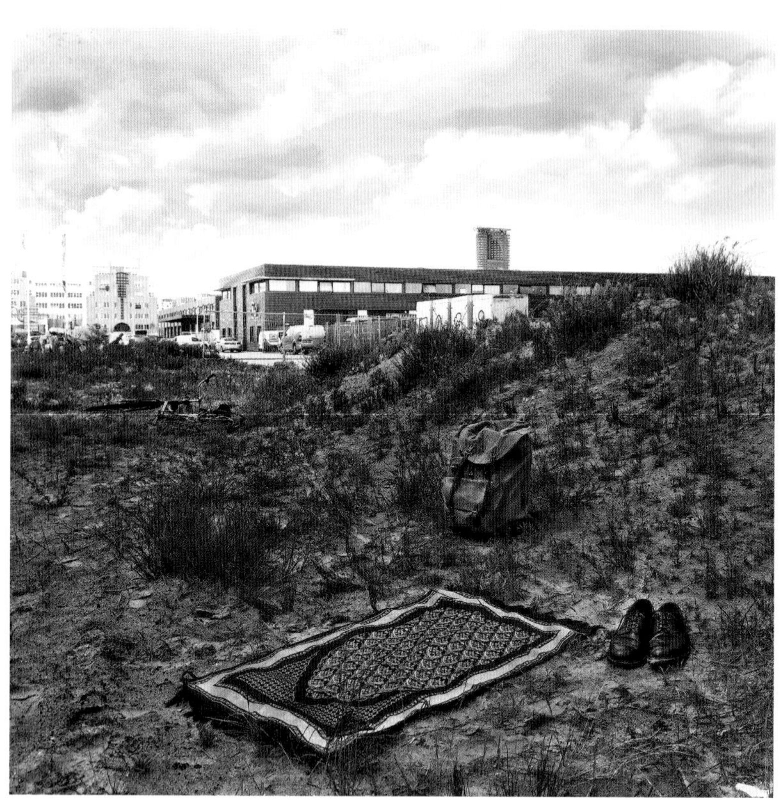

13:10:20, June 18th 2020. Binckhorst Wasteland, The Hague, Netherlands

For
how
l o n g
does a
prayer
exist?

Five times a day, no matter where he is,
Marwan Bassiouni unrolls his rug, lays it on the
ground facing Mecca, and prays. Afterward,
he stands up, takes a picture of the rug, and
later posts it on Instagram using the hashtag
#PrayerRugSelfie. His collection now exists
as an interactive map (marwanbassiouni.com/the-map). In some
pictures, the rug lies on the floor of a living room or bedroom.
Sometimes it is surrounded by space, or lies awkwardly in a corner,
between furniture, or across a narrow corridor. Sometimes the
rug appears outdoors, as if placed at random on a riverbank or
the tarmac of a parking lot. Compositionally, the angle of the rug
is always the same forty-five degrees; however, its placement in
relation to the environment is clearly dictated by something other
than the lines of architecture.

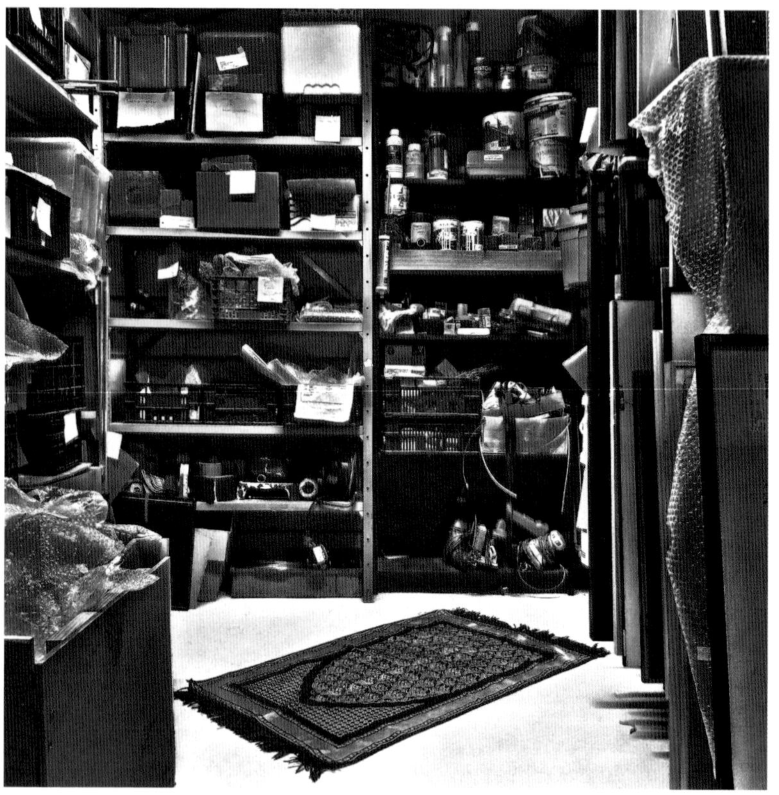

Though he does not appear in the images himself, Bassiouni's presence is felt, not only as the photographer, but through the evidence of his private act. His shoes and bag sometimes sit beside the rug, and the context, whether darkroom or kitchen, offers hints as to what daily activity his prayer has interrupted. For a few moments, banal outdoor locations and domestic interiors are transformed into precious sites of worship, before the rug is rolled up, causing the spaces to revert to their previous functions.

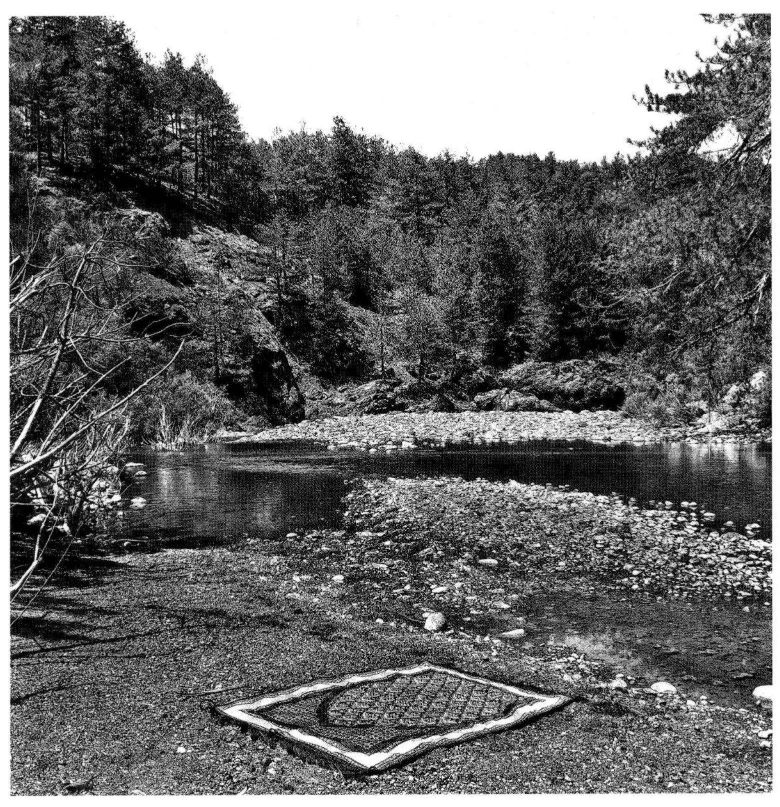

From one image to the next, the vacant rug becomes a kind
of island of Islamic faith surrounded by the practical necessities of
day-to-day life; an island that allows us to reflect on the sacro-
sanct yet intangible nature of faith. Bassiouni might have chosen
to show himself in the act of prayer—generally, photographers do
like to show us things—but somehow his physical absence more
deeply embodies his devotion to Islam. We are reminded that the
essence of what matters most is often invisible.

Opposite: *16:54:08, November 19th 2019. SBK Galerie, Amsterdam, The Netherlands*
Above: *14:00:34, July 21st 2019. Pindos National Park, Greece*

Is military service a form of worship?

In Kristine Potter's black-and-white photographs, young male cadets at West Point Military Academy wear combat gear, making them appear semitransparent against the landscape. Pictured in the midst of their four-year transformation from adolescent civilians into defenders of the nation, the cadets seem to be performing a slow, deliberate vanishing act, one that requires them to abandon their sense of individuality for the sake of merging into the corps. Permeating Potter's images is a sense of foreboding stillness, a calm before the storm. Unlike the up-close, raw depictions of bloodied soldiers on the front line photographed by the likes of Robert Capa and Don McCullin, Potter's images depict men who are yet to face the physical and psychological traumas of war. Their fates are unknown, their futures nascent. Occasionally, their gazes meet Potter's camera and we see glimpses of their youthful vulnerability and uncertainty about what might lie ahead; however, the individual behind the eyes is obscured by an ever-increasing dedication to duty and faith in a nation. These men are willing to give their lives for their country, and for that they must edge toward anonymity. In Potter's images, their ghostly presence elevates them into intangible, almost spiritual entities in which America places so much faith.

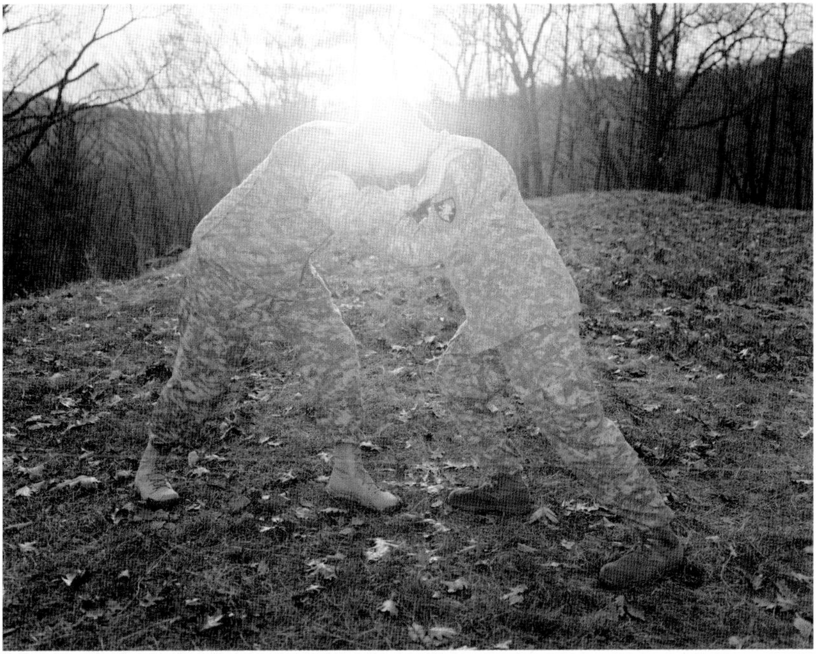

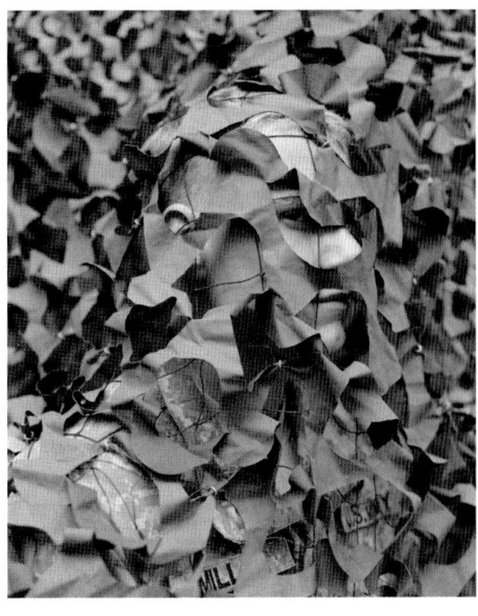

Above: Untitled, 2005–10

When we talk of God, could we be talking about the future of science?

"Freezer Failure Ends Couple's Hopes of Life after Death," ran the newspaper headline that prompted Murray Ballard to take a deeper look into the world of cryonics, the science of freezing a human body after death in the hope of one day bringing it back to life. The facilities in Ballard's photographs appear antiquated, and the doctors and lab technicians a little kooky as they pose outside garden sheds and act out training exercises in suburban driveways. In other images, the earnestness of the prospective patients is on display; the fading few possessions of those already frozen stir melancholy. In one sense, this version of life after death seems utterly bonkers, while at the same time wholly rational and optimistic. That combination of descriptors—bonkers, rational, and optimistic—could be used to describe our underlying commitments to any faith. It is bonkers to believe in a God and equally bonkers to believe in the possibilities of unproven science; it is entirely rational to believe in a God or the possibilities of science if it soothes your fear of death; believing that death is only the beginning is, in many ways, the logical extreme of optimism. By depicting these doctors as suspect divinities and their patients as their faithful supplicants, Ballard's deep dive into the world of cryonics suggests that religious and scientific faiths are not the opposites we are often led to believe they are. Let us pray for the sake of the frozen that their gods—future humans—do indeed possess the power of resurrection.

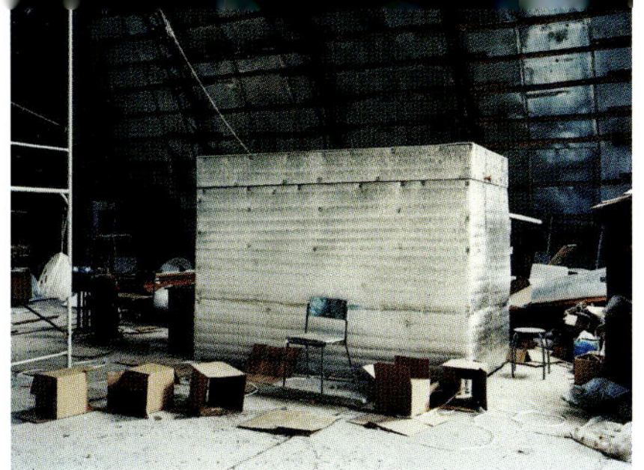

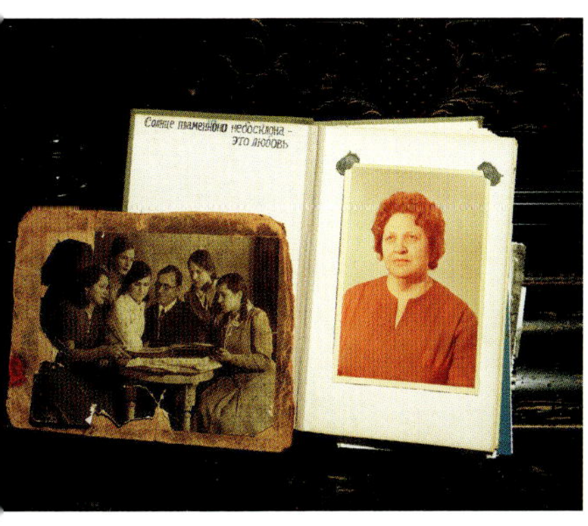

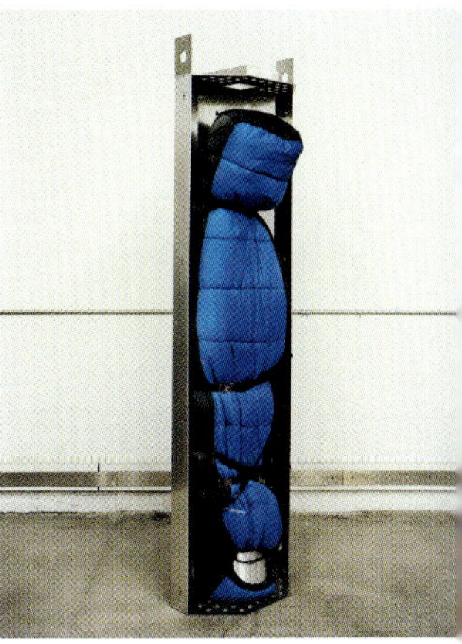

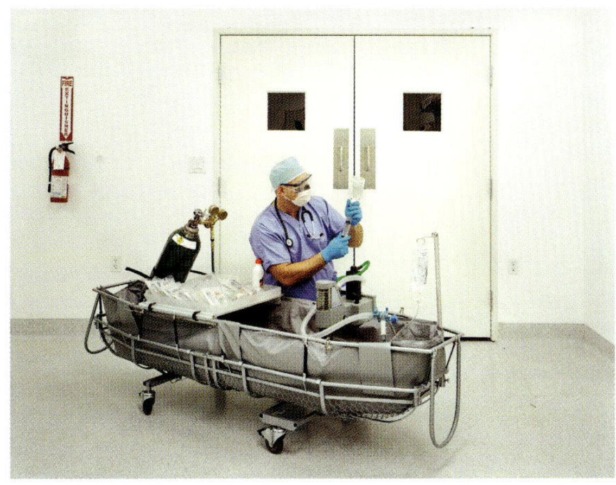

Photos from the series *The Prospect of Immortality*, 2006–16

CON

There are some things people say that you never forget. No doubt you can recall one such example now. A remark that comes to mind for me involved two women who were, at the time, closest to me: my first girlfriend and my mother. I was twenty and I had just been dumped—like the worst kind of dumped. My mother was consoling me on the sofa, listening attentively to my streaming disbelief about being abandoned by another woman. I can't remember exactly what she had said up to that point; no doubt she offered up platitudes about time and healing, and these things making me stronger. But what-ever she had said, it wasn't working, and after an hour or so, I could tell she was getting a little fidgety. That's when she lifted her arm from around my shoulders, stood up, and said, "Darling, you need to understand some-thing: We all die alone." And with that, she left the room to feed the dogs.

Her words wounded me like the snip-ping of an umbilical cord. In a strange, unconscious, Freudian sort of way, I think this was her final act of releas-ing me, a scolding baptism into a cruel and tender world where I would have to accept that love is not always unconditional, that the only relation-ship that will remain until the very end is the one I have with myself. I'd like to say that I was hit by an epiphany, that her words instantly solved the problem. But, of course, love and loss are not that simple, not that logical, which is why they preoccupy not just artists, but all of us.

CONNECTION

In this section, the photographers draw on their own experiences to try to make sense of a human need that's as fundamental to us as food: our compulsion to form deep, emotional connections with others, even if it means changing aspects of ourselves and risking debilitating grief. Whether responding to familial relationships we are born into, or relationships we form with strangers who later become friends or lovers, this work is, at times, as comforting as it is confronting. The photographers reflect on the complex psychological interplay between children and parents and the politics that creep into sexual partnerships. Some work finds hope in moments of national tragedy and strength in personal loss; some responds to the COVID-19 pandemic lockdowns, a time that has reminded us how much we need human connection. Dig deep enough into this work and you will unearth insights into universal quandaries that we all have to grapple with from conception to coffin: Who makes me who I am? Where is the boundary between myself and others? How do I navigate the line between dependence and autonomy? Am I really going to die alone?

This work is, at times, as comforting as it is confronting.

What should
a mother
think when
she holds her
child?

Here, the bond between mother and daughter is expressed in swelling and narrowing lines traveling down the image. If this flow of vulva-like forms were extended lengthways, one could imagine the composition growing into a never-ending pattern of mother, daughter, mother, daughter. But why is the woman turned toward the open door, and is the daughter playing with her mother's hair or clinging to it? Mixing staged photographs of nonrelatives and observed moments of family members, Lindley Warren Mickunas delves into the complexities lurking within the most universal connection of them all—the maternal bond. Her photographic process is a form of "psychodrama," a psychoanalytic technique that uses role-play and reenactments to gain insights into one's past. The stylistically detached nature of her setups and use of stark, isolating flash creates hard-to-decipher images that are tender and violent, warm and cool.

Visualizations of distant memories are interwoven with Warren Mickunas's own anxieties about the prospect of motherhood to create a perspective that shifts between that of an infant and that of a parent. Are the adult hands resting on a boy's shoulders providing comfort or serving to oppress? Is the milk dripping from rubber gloves, squeezed like udders, a product of play or of violence? Quite unlike typical depictions of parenthood, such as the idyllic paintings of Madonna and Child dating back to Raphael and the Renaissance, and more recent representations proliferated by social media matriarchs today, Warren Mickunas's photographs peels back the layers of sentimentality that so often conceal the taut, push-pull tensions of the familial bond.

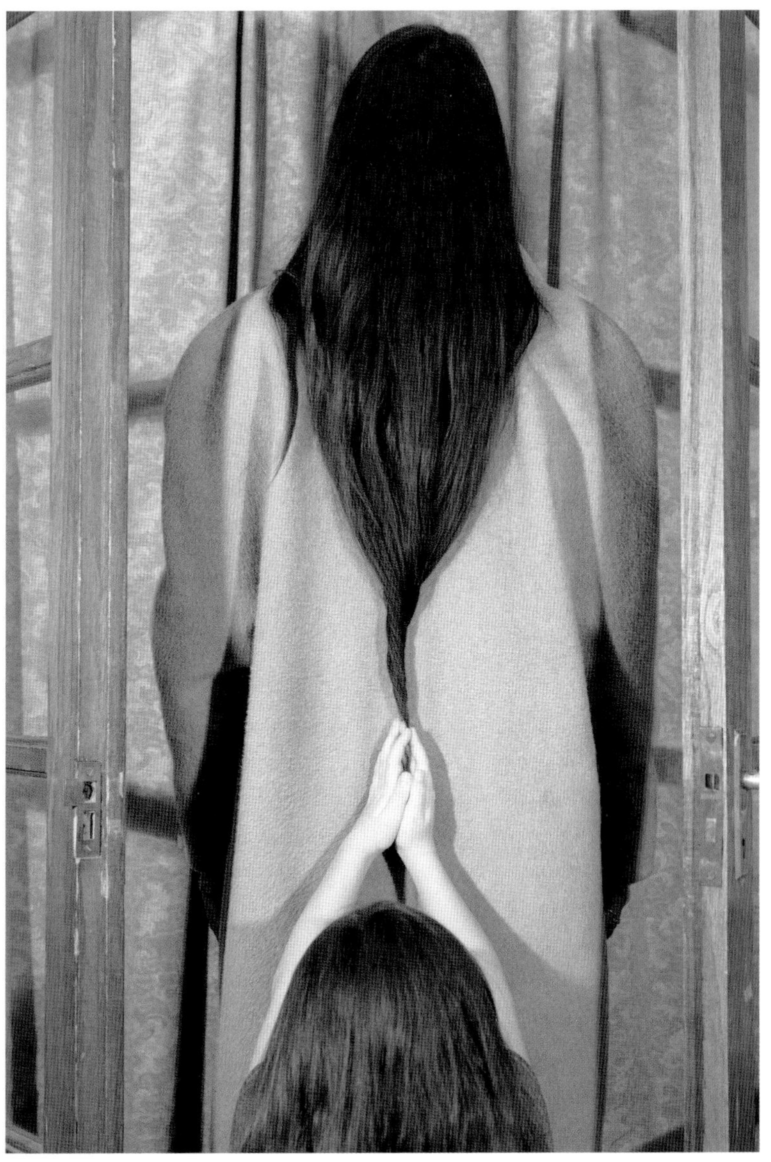

Mother and Daughter, 2017

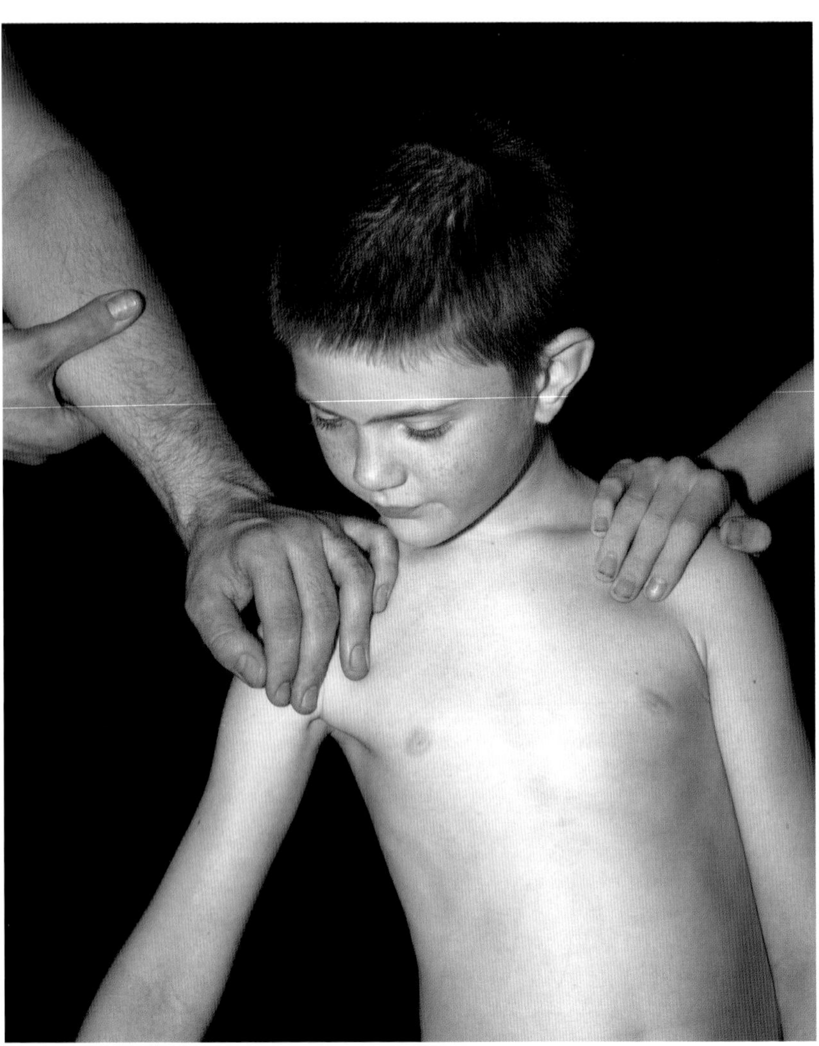

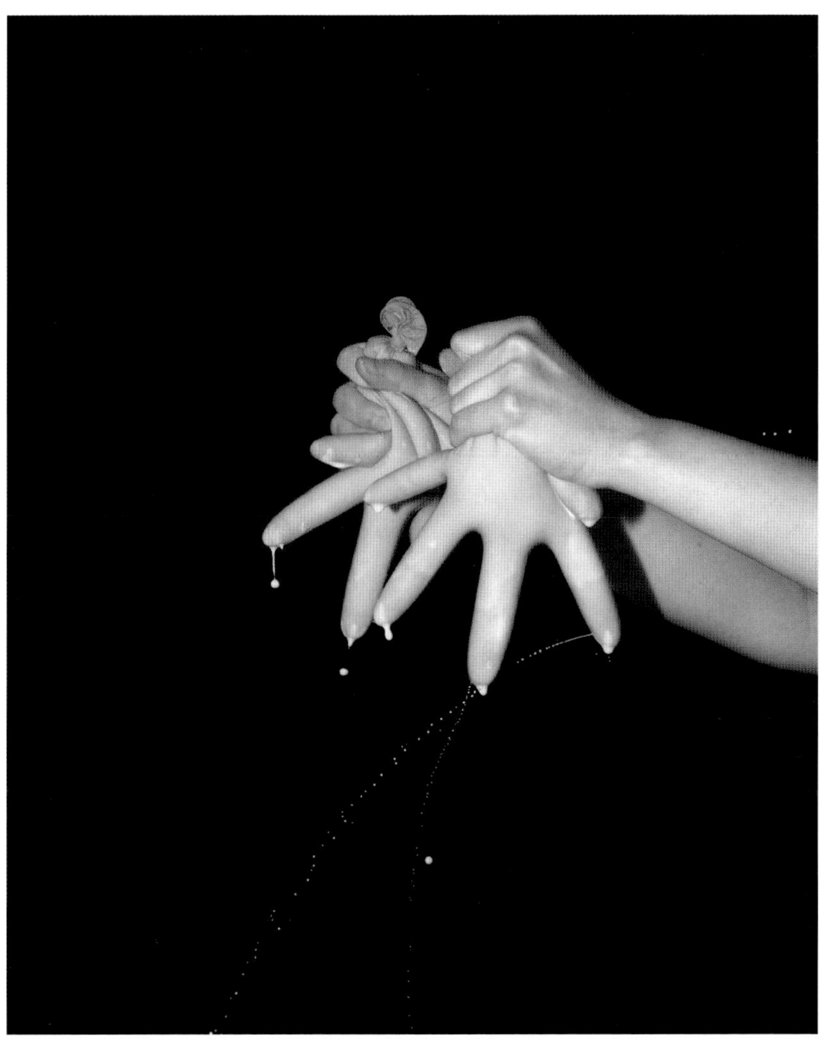

Opposite: *Three Hands*, 2019 | Above: *Milk*, 2020

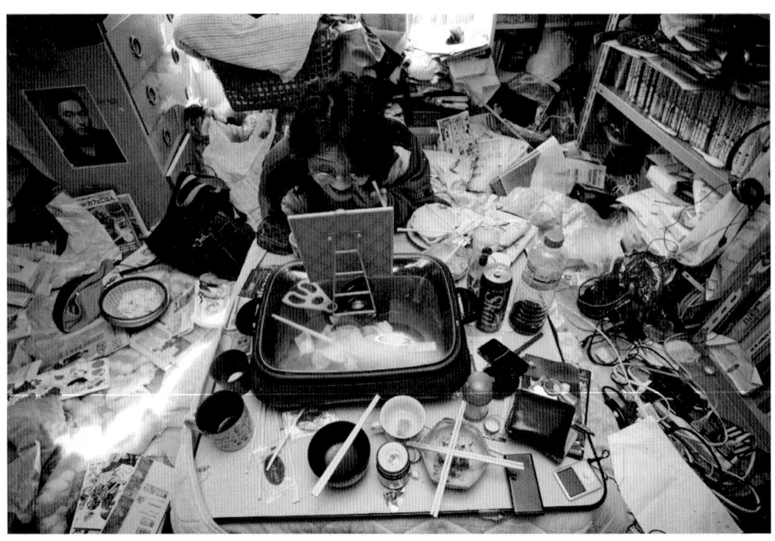

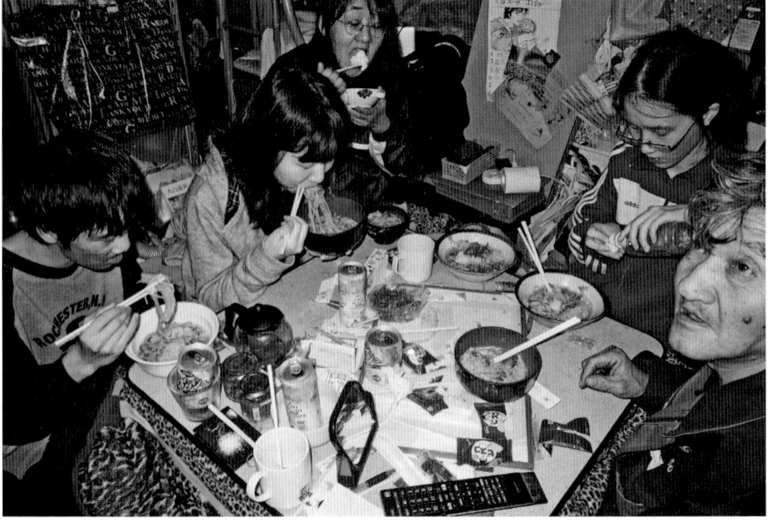

Top: *Guts #10*, 2014–17
Bottom: *Guts #34*, 2014–17

Do you feel closer to people when they are closer?

Just imagine it. A family of seven cohabiting for eighteen years in a tiny one-room apartment. This was reality for Masaki Yamamoto, whose aptly named series Guts depicts his parents and siblings trying to stay on top of, quite literally, their ever-accumulating clutter. Here, no inch of domestic or compositional space is spared, and we, too, are pulled into their cramped quarters and forced to visually tiptoe through the mess. With no doors to lock, with no bedrooms to sulk in, privacy is a privilege not afforded to Yamamoto's family, which is perhaps why their chaotic dysfunction is played out, without inhibition, in front of the camera. Mundane moments are amplified, not only because everyone is captured up close, but because we can almost hear the visual commotion from one picture to the next. Yet despite the circumstances, Yamamoto's photographs show the humor, tenderness, and affection that his family members have for one another. Rather than coming across as destitute, they appear resilient; Mother uses a hot plate as a makeup table, Father stands in the kitchen shaving his head in his underpants. Within these four smoke-stained walls, no family member eludes Yamamoto's lens. Depicted in the reductive tones of black and white, people and place are fused, and claustrophobia is a housemate. Everyone and everything become visually inseparable.

How have you
dealt with
the traumas
of your
childhood?

For Jonny Briggs, splicing together photographs of his family is a way of making sense or reclaiming control of his childhood, one overshadowed by an emotionally distant, alcoholic father and a staunchly religious education. Briggs's playful and obsessive morphing of his parents' physical forms creates unnerving, surreal visions. In one assemblage, his father's reptilian hand grows from Briggs's mother's neck, obscuring her vision. In another, Briggs's mother's manicured fingertips pierce a childhood photograph of her husband. And in another, four photographs, each taken from a slightly different angle, form an image of his mother's head, yet her features are concealed by the stark, crosshair-like lines of the grid. Briggs's depictions are full of religious, sexual, and authoritarian symbolism, yet what rises to the surface is influenced not so much by his feelings toward his family as by the peculiarities of human history. After all, what is normal when it comes to family?

I wondered what Mr. and Mrs. Briggs made of their son's creations. Briggs told me that his mother is supportive, while his father is less open about his feelings, standing in front of Briggs's images largely silent. This knowledge can lend an unintended significance to the artworks. Their reception must feed back into the family dynamic, adding complication or clarity about what has occurred. That is the brave and difficult thing about making work that comments on one's relationship to living parents. Whatever manifests itself visually acts as a mirror that's been given its own place setting at the dinner table.

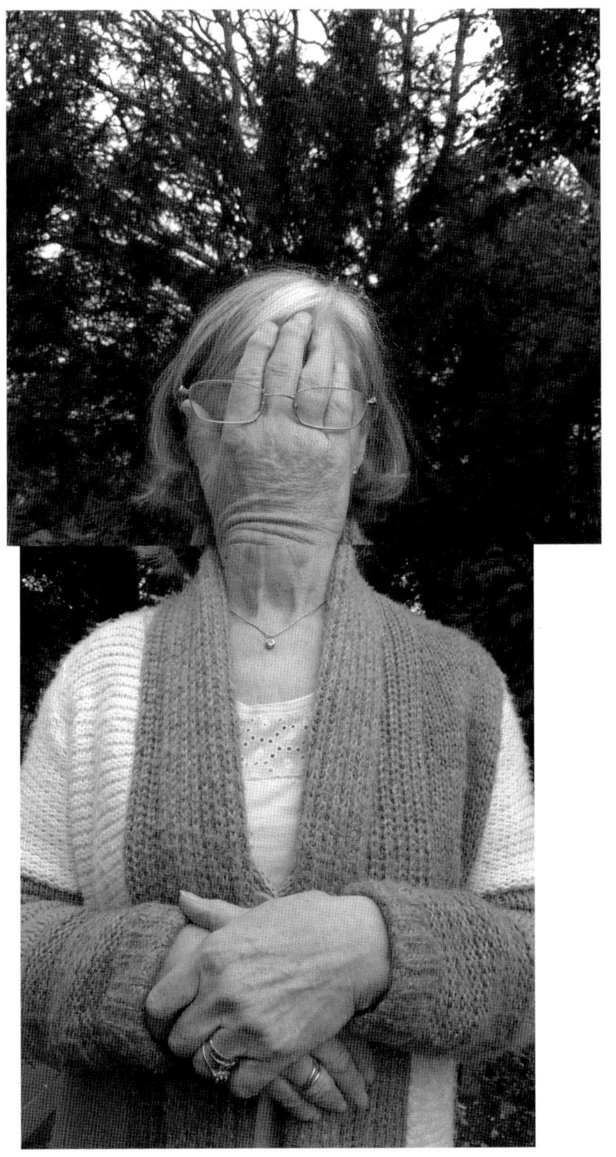

My Blood, 2017

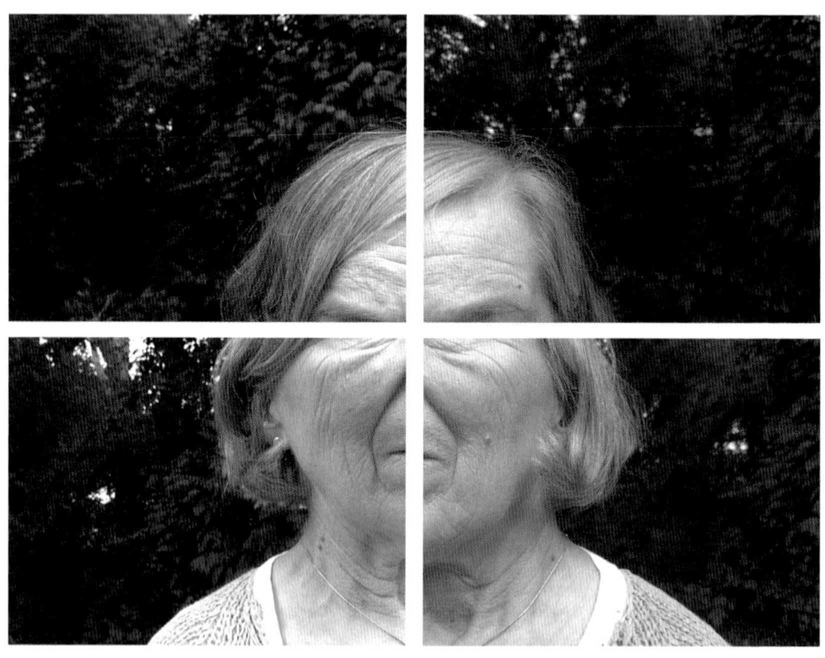

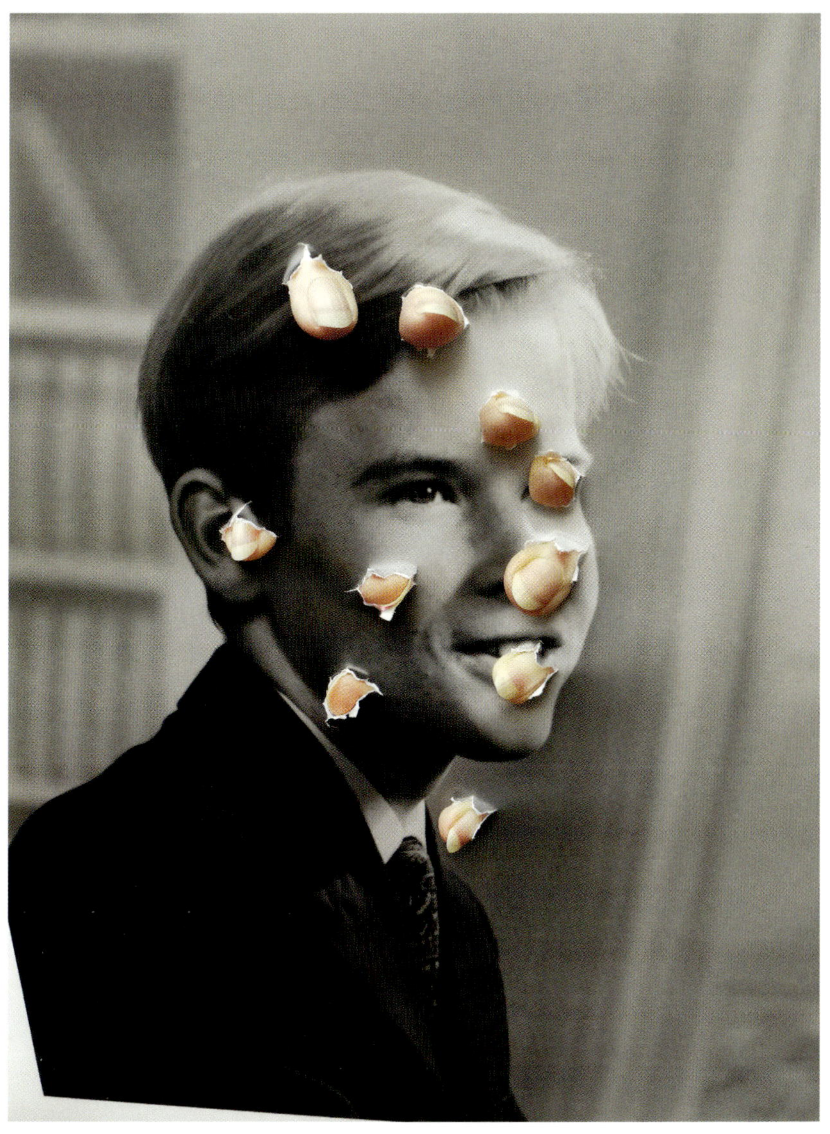

Opposite: *A Window In To / Out Of*, 2016 | Above: *Consuming a Grief That's Yet to Come*, 2017

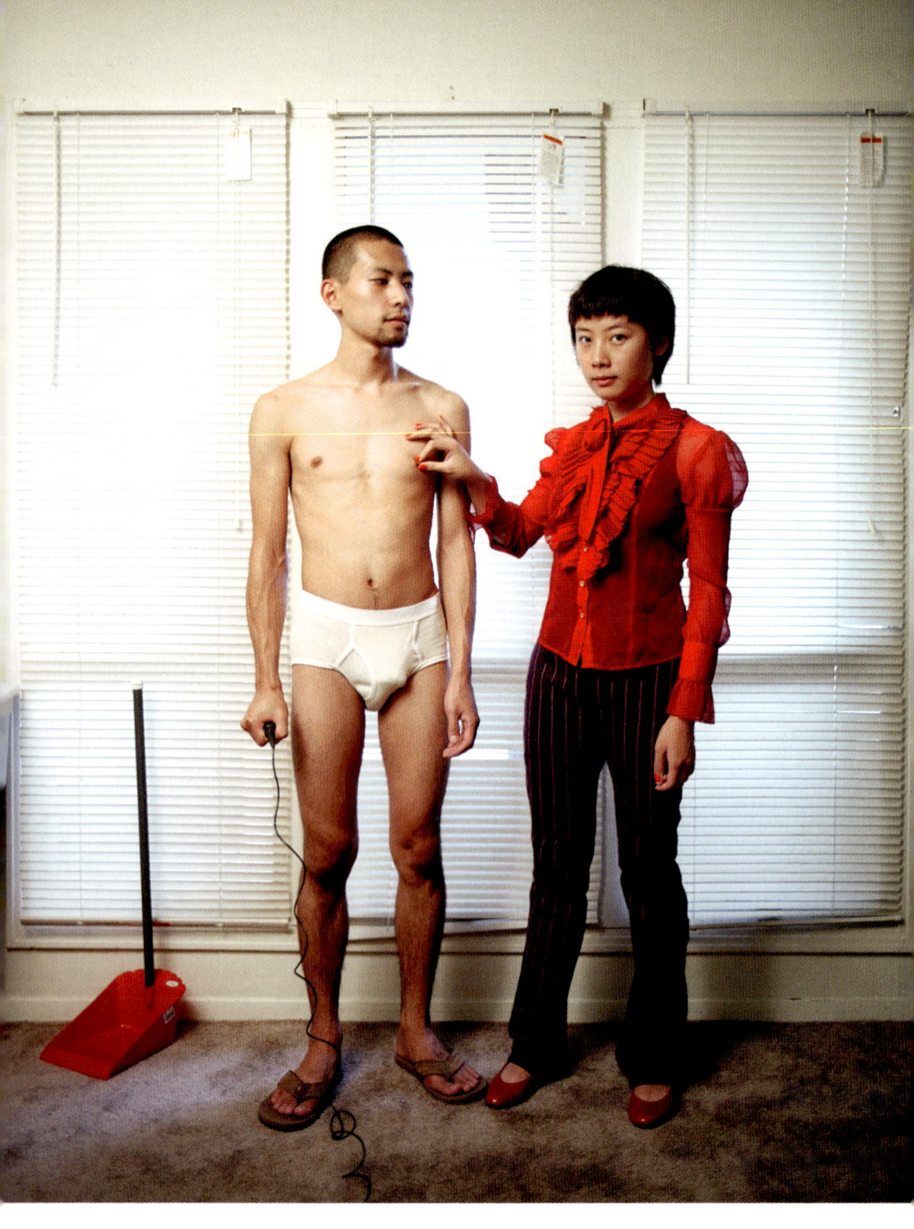

Relationships Work Best When Each Partner Knows Their Proper Place, 2008

He may be the one squeezing the cable release, but she is pinching his nipple. His attention is channeled at her; she stares at us. His briefs do little to protect his modesty; she is dressed in vivacious red, as if about to leave for work. And what's with that dustpan? This ambiguous portrait clearly nods to historical paintings about the desire, control, and sexuality of romantic partnerships. The world's most famous nipple tweak comes to mind as seen in the painting *Gabrielle d'Estrées and One of Her Sisters* by an unknown artist, as does the pitchfork-wielding farmer and his wife in Grant Wood's *American Gothic*. Here, the "she" in the photograph is the artist, Pixy Liao, and the "he" is Moro, her longtime model and boyfriend.

Is a relationship ever "healthy"?

Liao, originally from China, was brought up to believe that women should seek older male partners to mentor and protect them. Yet when she met and fell in love with Moro, who is five years her junior, her concept of a romantic relationship changed; Liao had more power, experience, and authority than her lover, and so began her ongoing project Experimental Relationship. Sometimes Moro is treated like a doll or pet, dressed up like a sushi roll, or hanging off a coat rail. In another staged image he lies on the dining table with half a papaya covering his genitals. Some scenes are tender, picturing the two of them in bed or embracing, but there is always a slight tension between them—Moro is always a little at Liao's mercy.

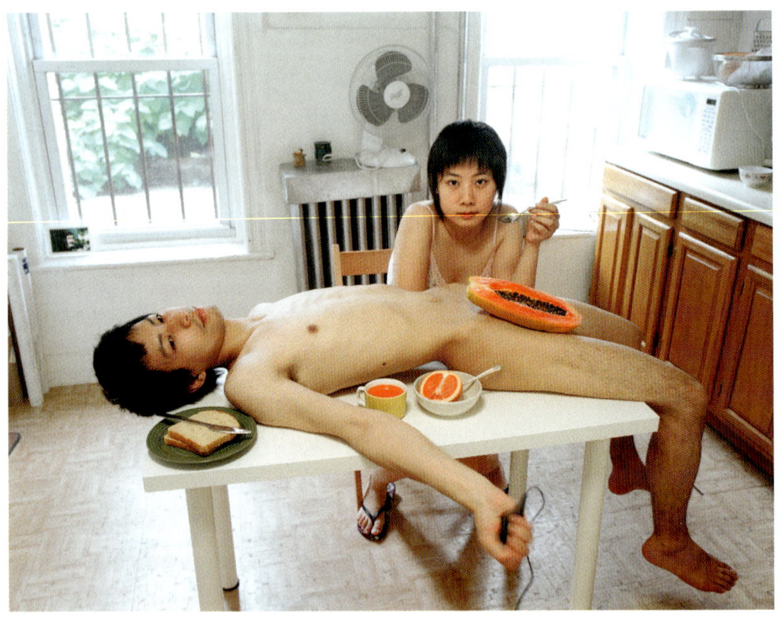

If we didn't know he was a willing participant in his girlfriend's artistic antics, we might feel sorry for him; we might look at this as a form of domestic abuse. But clearly this is, for both of them, a perfectly volitional fetish, one that challenges the traditional dynamics of a heterosexual relationship. We, too, become participants, endeared and amused by the ongoing performance. Yet if we stop to consider what is so comically

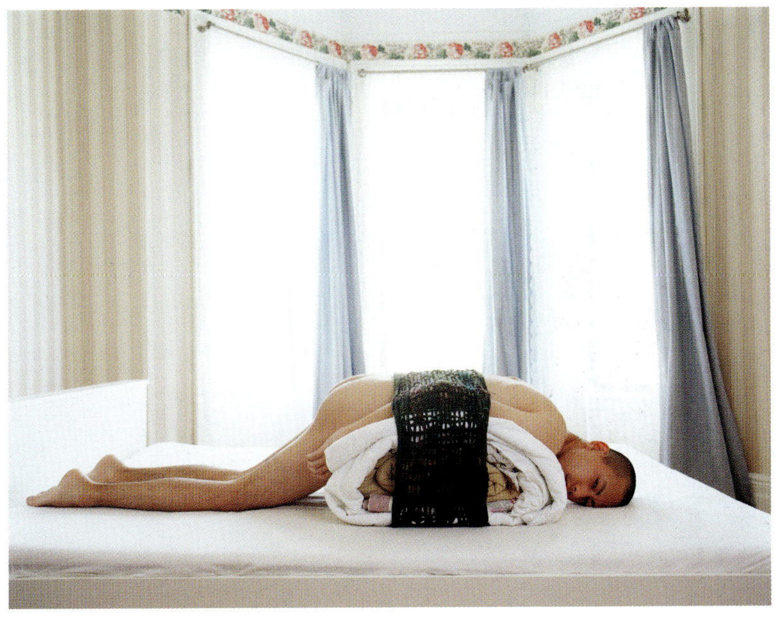

absurd about Liao's subversive work, we are met with a realization
that it is not their role-play that is so peculiar, even uncomfortable
at times—it's our own. How is your partner supposed to act? What
needs are they supposed to fulfill? With Experimental Relationship,
Liao makes fun of the political, cultural, and social expectations
that infiltrate romantic relationships, particularly when it comes to
the traditions of domestic partnerships.

Opposite: *Start Your Day with a Good Breakfast Together*, 2009 | Above: *Homemade Sushi*, 2010

**LUIS ALBERTO
RODRIGUEZ**

During a residency in southeast Ireland, Luis Alberto Rodriguez, a former dancer, became fascinated by the beauty of human movement in hurling, an ancient and brutal game said to predate Christianity. Rodriguez photographed the players in choreographed "scrums." He chose to do this off the pitch, in farmyards and other places that provide a backdrop of rural industry. Bodies become physically entangled into a single conglomerate, literally bonded as a team and metaphorically tied to an ancient pastime. Though the bodies of these young men are powerful and supple, there is also tenderness in their fresh faces and a sense of precious kinship in their uninhibited display of physical interdependence. In other images, Rodriguez presents us with tonal close-ups of exposed skin covered with mud, cuts, scrapes, and scars, which may have been caused by past clashes on or off the field. Homoerotic? A little. But that's just an inherent aspect of the male-on-male gaze. Rodriguez's primary fascination is with the exploration of time and place through human physicality. If it weren't for the modern sportswear, these abstract poses, captured in the timeless tones of black and white, could have been struck in this same location, by countless generations, stretching back thousands of years. With People of the Mud, Rodriguez offers up a tactile interpretation of how our bodies tie us to the past, how they give us a sense of groundedness and belonging to people and to place. History, physicality, landscape, and kinship become entwined.

Did your life begin before your birth?

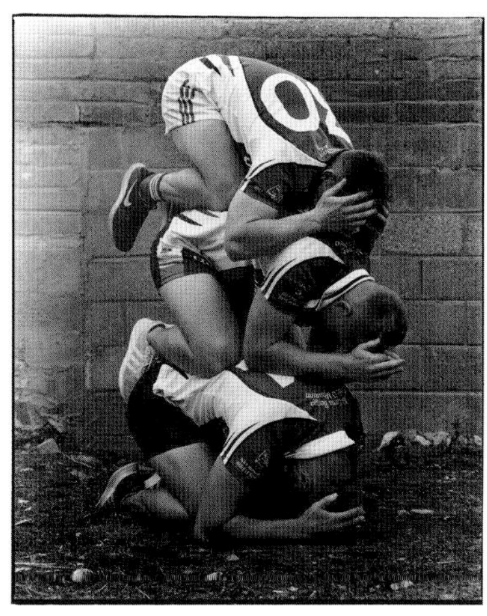

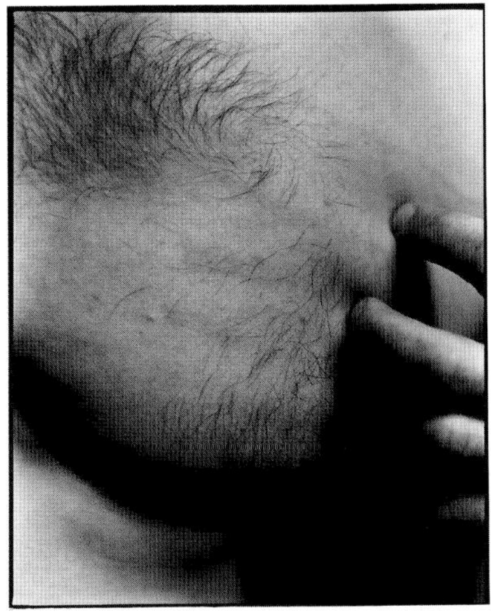

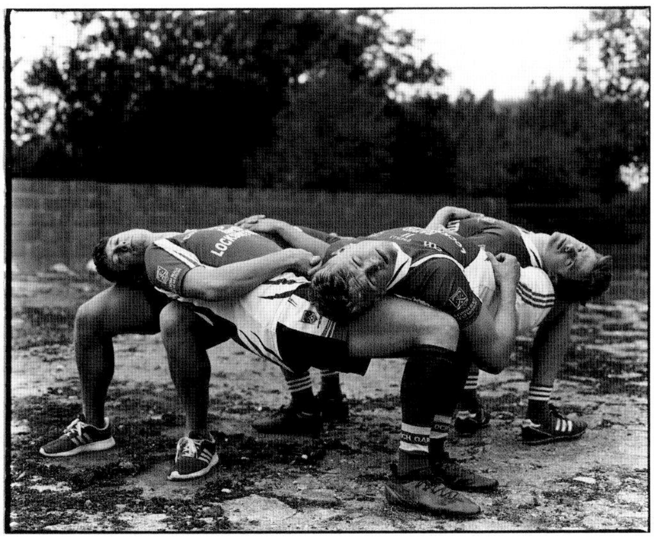

Above: Photos from the series People of the Mud, 2020

**ANDRES
GONZALEZ**

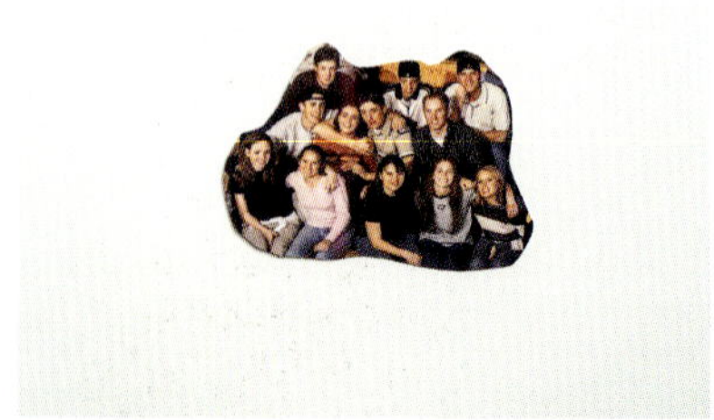

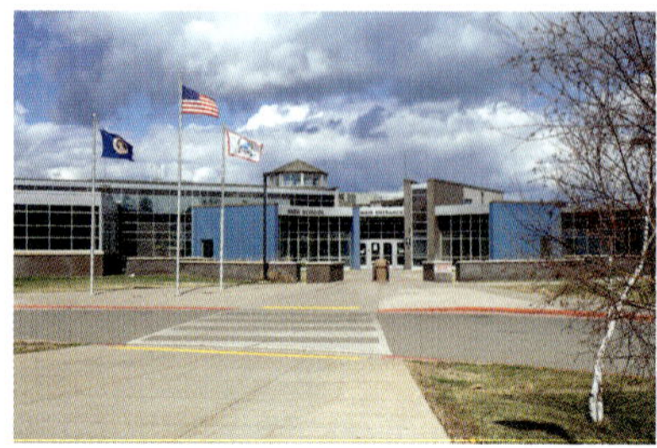

Can
Trauma
be inherited?

Following a school shooting, the school is inundated with
letters and gifts from people all over the world who share the
community's grief. Tens of thousands of teddy bears, religious
statues, handwritten cards, and photographs are stored in local
libraries. In some cases, the volume of material is so large that
eventually it has to be burned, its ashes preserved or scattered
as sacred soil. Following the Sandy Hook shooting in 2012,
Andres Gonzalez began visiting communities that had endured
the unbearable trauma of school shootings. He interviewed

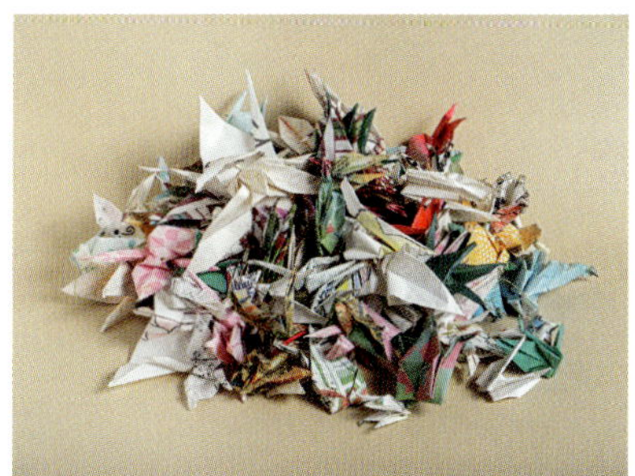

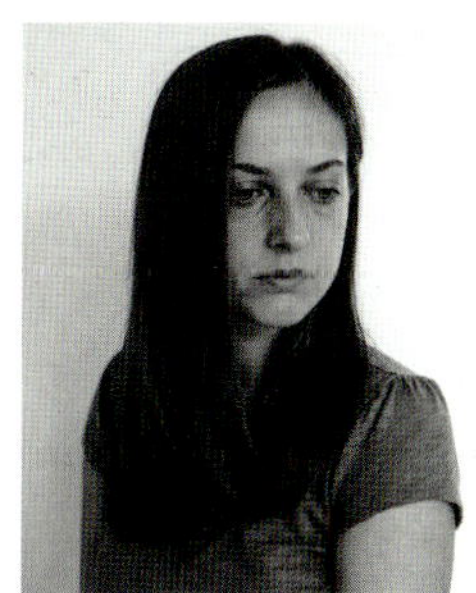

survivors, collected artifacts from the schools and students, and photographed the archives of condolences and the landscapes surrounding the schools. He then presented his research and photographs in a limited-edition photobook called American Origami, the name inspired by the folded paper cranes that symbolize hope in the face of trauma.

In contrast to the rawness and urgency of news footage, one might view Gonzalez's photographs as lacking life, compassion even. But they are not. Alongside the outpouring of emotion

This spread and following: Photos from the series American Origami, 2019

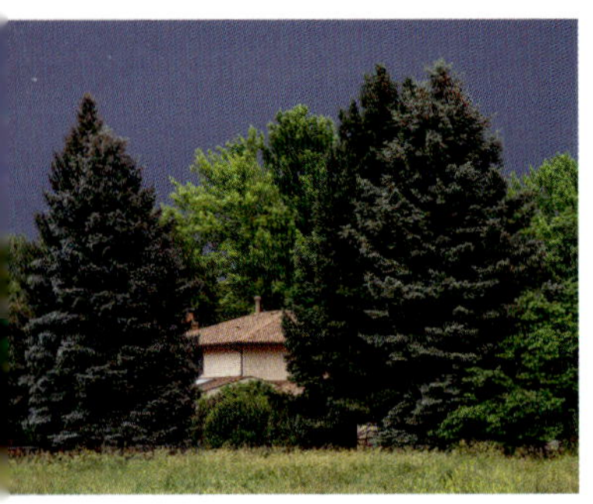

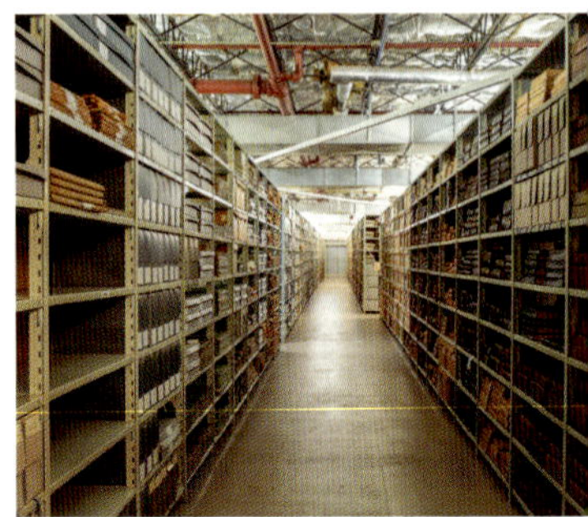

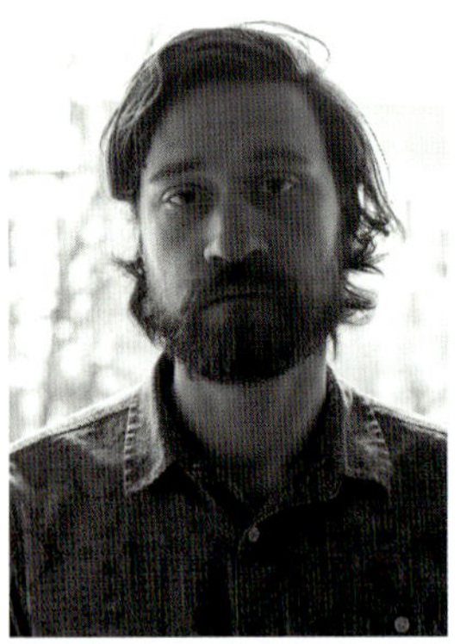

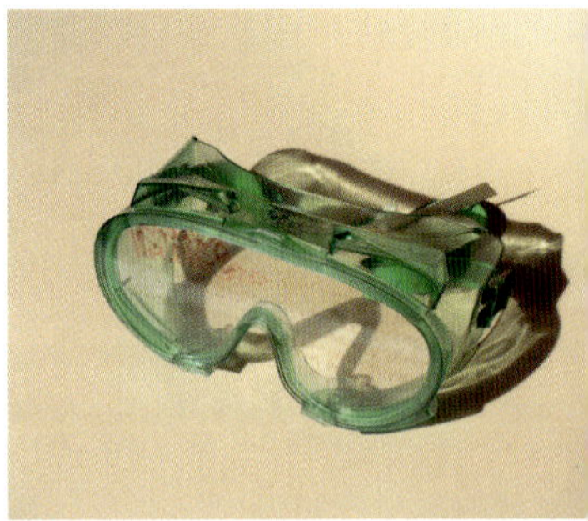

contained in the letters, Gonzalez's photographs of nondescript homes, desolate playing fields, and empty suburban streets offer us an opportunity for peaceful reflection, windows into grieving communities still coming to terms with the violence that transformed them into the epicenters of pain. Our experience of school shootings is shaped by the news footage, the drama and confusion, the horror and shock of it all, as captured at the scene. With American Origami, Gonzalez shows us images of the

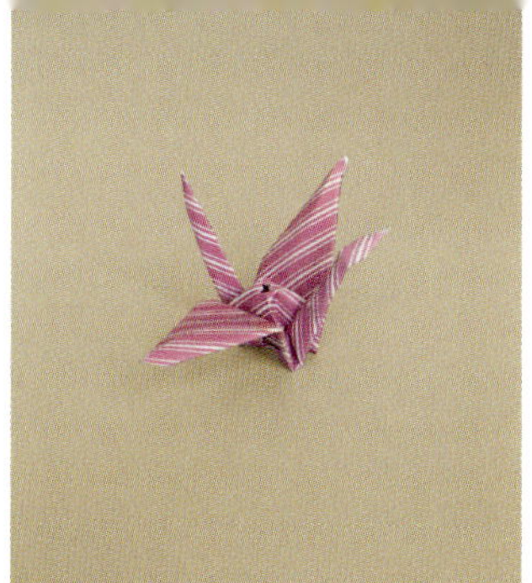

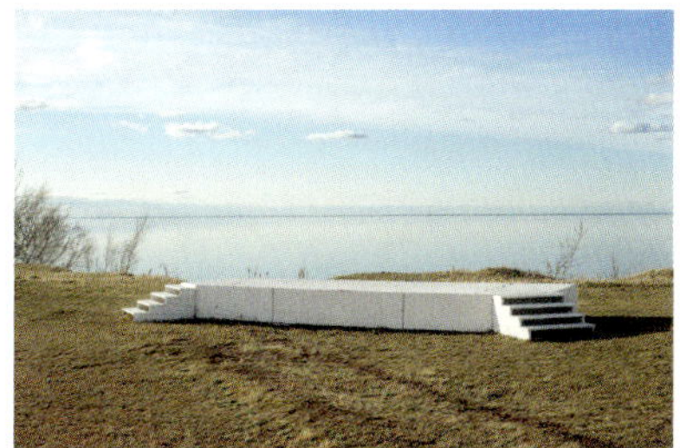

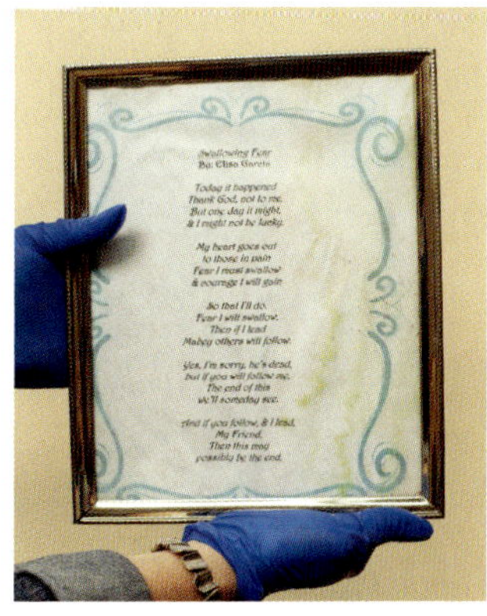

settled dust—the legacy of the wound. He shows us what happens to broken communities after the news cameras leave and the messages from grieving strangers are sealed in boxes. As much as we want, or need, to respond and make sense of events as they happen, Gonzalez's slow, unobtrusive images and almost forensic archive of loss show us that the extent of the wound reveals itself only with time.

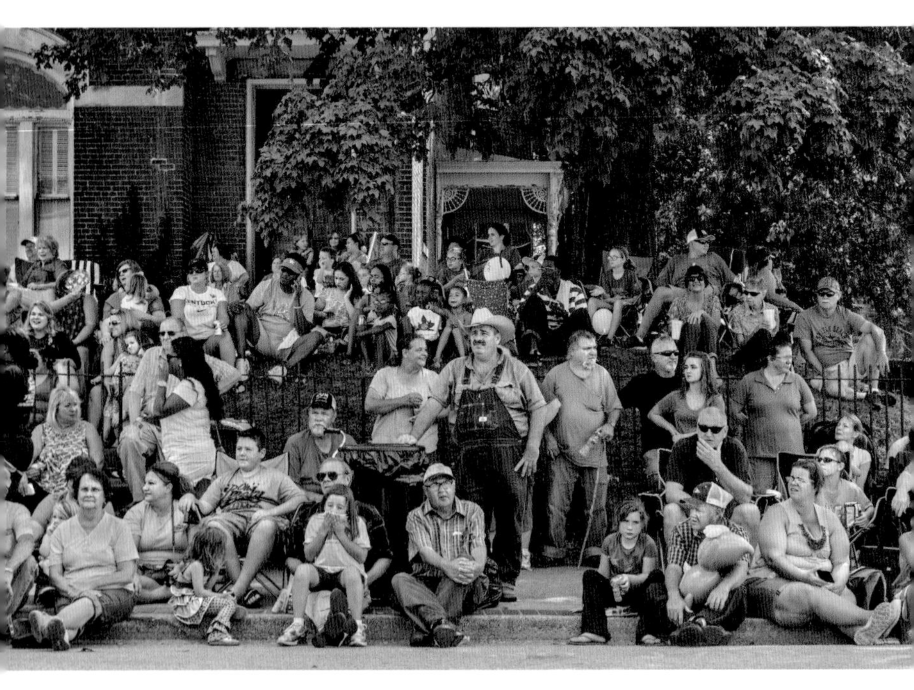

Above: *Marion County Country Ham Days, Pigasus Parade, Lebanon, Kentucky, September 24, 2016*
Following spread: *The Charro Days Fiesta parade in Brownsville, Tex.; Feb. 27, 2016*

Are strangers similar to you, or fundamentally different?

Some of the people in George Georgiou's tableaux may be stand-ing at opposite sides of the frame, but within the compositions they are totally dependent on one another. Each person, each tiny gesture, contributes to the rhythm of the scene, a part of the whole. In 2016, one of the most divisive years in recent American history, which saw, among other things, Donald Trump's election, Georgiou traveled the country photographing people at parades. The parades were not political; some celebrated Independence Day, others cranberries, and in each of these images, the event itself is not featured. What the people are gathered to witness becomes an unseen spectacle, a force that has pulled *them* together and turned them into the spectacle.

Often, a small detail would catch Georgiou's eye, prompting him to take the photograph. Only afterward does the full richness of what he has captured emerge from the stillness of the image.

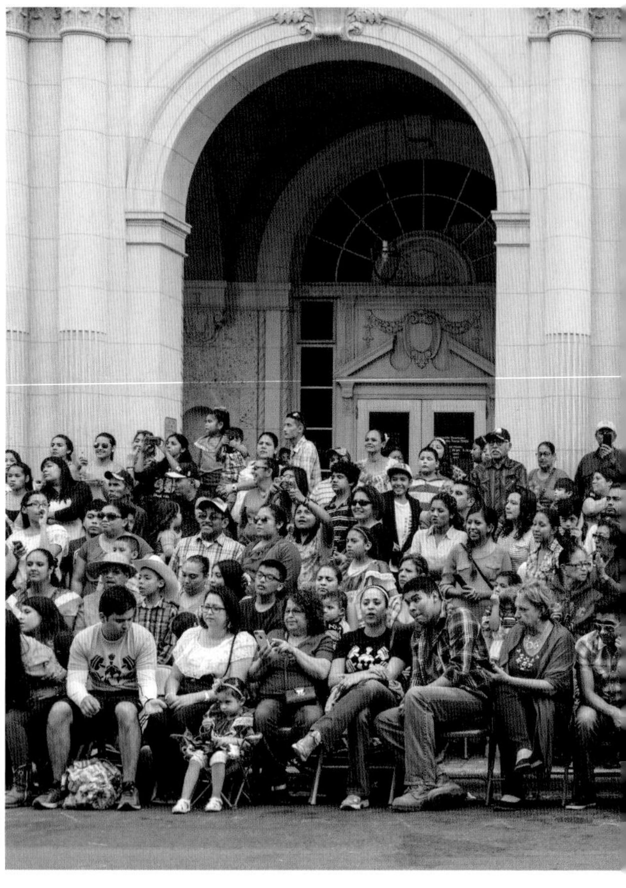

The photograph on page 88, taken in Kentucky, shows a gathering of people waiting for a parade celebrating their community's love of ham. Starting with the plump man in the center, our eyes ricochet around the scene, latching onto one person, one detail, and then darting to the next. The image is alive with gestures, expressions, and glances. Little pockets of anticipation, boredom, and malaise ebb and flow in a composition that makes it impossible

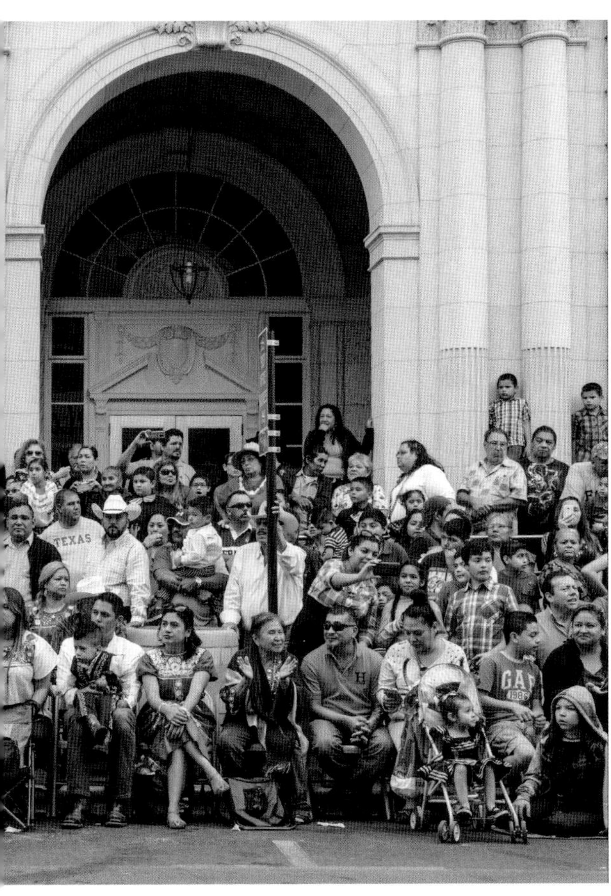

to tell which of the subjects are friends and which are strangers
to each other. In an era when we choose to stand increasingly
apart, to distance ourselves from people with different views (not
to mention the social distancing ushered in by the pandemic), the
people in Georgiou's compositions are wonderfully unified. No
matter who they are and what they believe, all that matters is the
passing parade.

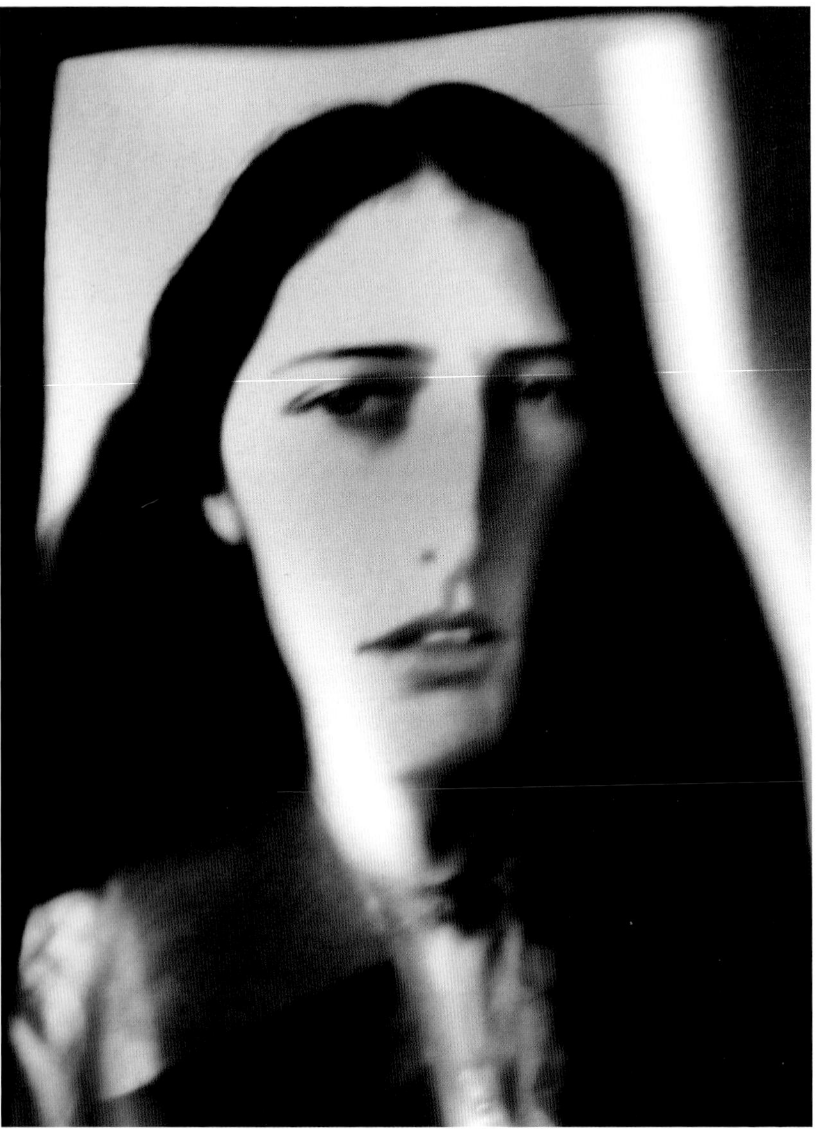

Untitled, 2020

What do photographers do when the world denies them the raw ingredient they need to create work—a physical subject? During lockdown, in response to this very particular problem, Jack Davison made ethereal portraits by photographing projected images of his video calls with friends and relatives. Sometimes he introduced additional layers of obstruction, such as a piece of glass placed between projector and image, to heighten the sense of separation from his subjects. Though they draw on a modern technological innovation—live video calls—these blurry, black-and-white images feel more like products of early photographic technology. The camera obscura, for instance, projects an image of the outside world into a darkened room by allowing light to travel through a hole in a wall covered by a simple lens. Not only do Davison's portraits speak to the feeling of disconnection that many of us have so profoundly felt during self-isolation, they also reflect the duality embedded in photography itself.

Photography is a medium unlike any other in that it relies on the physical presence of someone or something to create an image that is, however, entirely separate or removed from its subject. The people in Davison's photographs appear like ghosts. And in many ways, that is what photography does best: create ghosts, incarnations of people who are not there. During the COVID-19 pandemic, to maintain our connection with those we love most, we have transformed ourselves into images and, in the eyes of others, ceased to exist in physical terms. We have become ghosts in order to remain in one another's lives.

Do you need to be seen to feel like you exist?

Does a photograph change when its subject dies?

It started with a good-bye. As Deanna Dikeman left her parents' house after a regular visit in July 1991, she snapped a picture. Her mother stands in the foreground, her fuchsia blouse and blue shorts vivid in the sunlight, the tilt of her body full of life, her hand raised as in a high five. In the background, a man stands in the shade of a tree, striking an almost identical pose, just a little stiffer: Dikeman's father. From that moment on, Dikeman took a photograph every time she left her parents' house, a habit that lasted another twenty-six years. Some of the resulting images are full of joy, the kind of default happiness that runs through family members when everything's good, not much to report. In others, Dikeman's aging parents seem a little preoccupied. Her mother, especially, has that look that follows someone saying, "Don't worry, I'm sure it's nothing." Years flip by, reduced to a few images; time seems to exert a stronger pull on Dad. We know what is coming, and when we reach an image of Mom standing alone, we know what has happened. Dikeman's reflection in the wing mirror of the car suggests that it's just the two of them now. A flurry of color images tries to suppress the grief, and Mom puts on a brave face in her trademark fuchsia and blue. Life goes on. Seasons pass. But that arm isn't held quite so high anymore. The good-byes seem a little more significant. The frequency of Dikeman's visits increases. The family home is substituted for a care home. A portrait of Mom and son. A final image of the house. Leaves on the driveway. The garage door closed. There is no one waving goodbye.

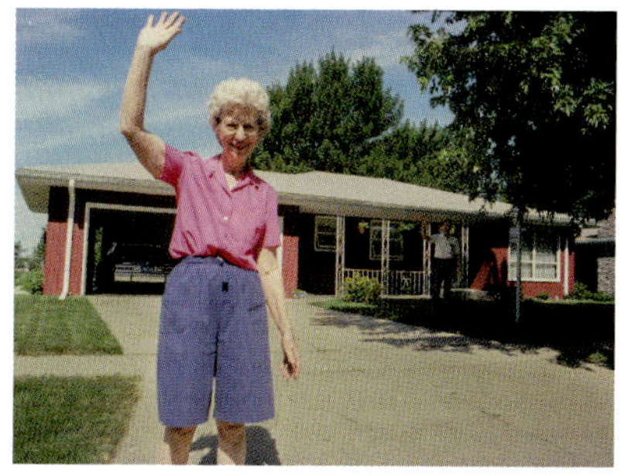
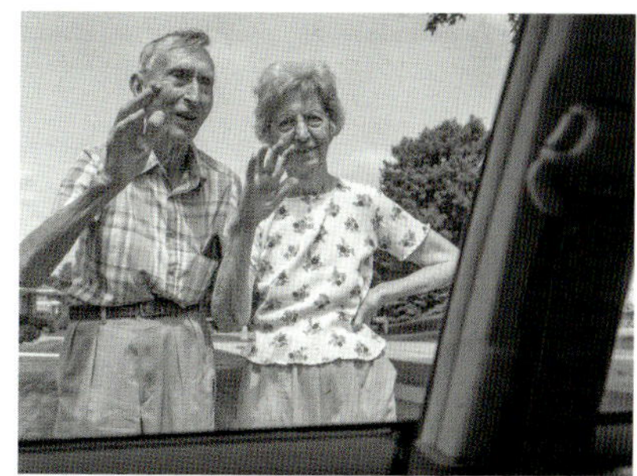
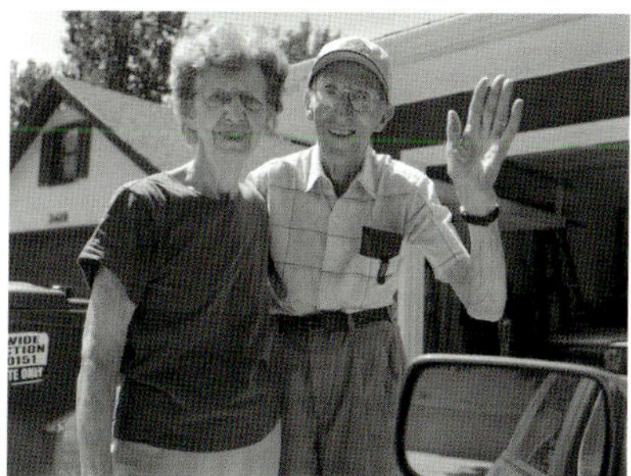
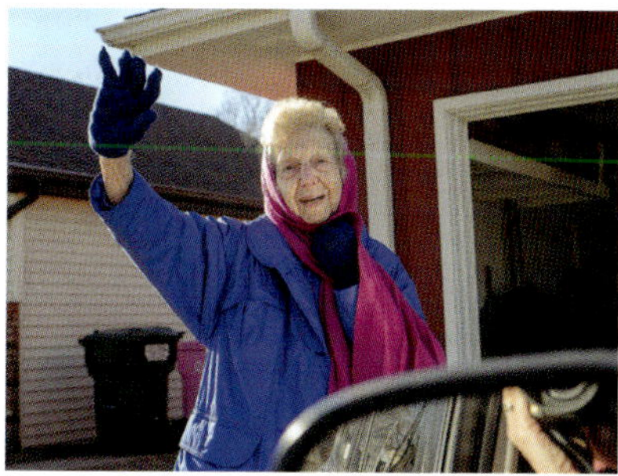
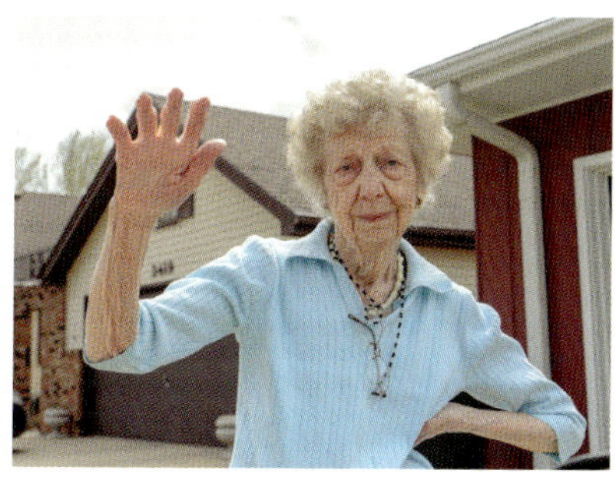
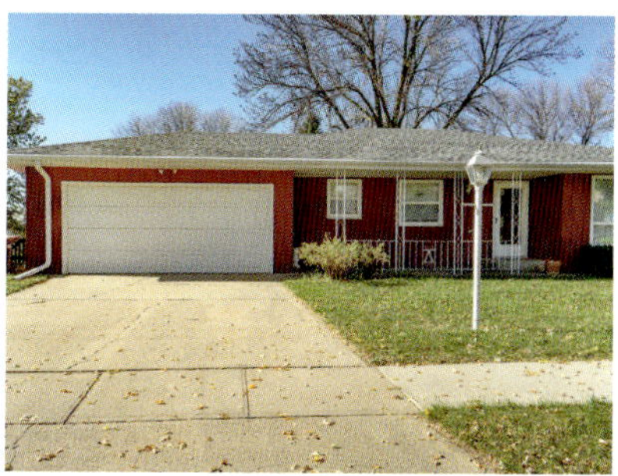

Photos from the series Leaving and Waving, 1991–2017

DIVI

The work in this section responds to the abject cruelty of human nature, cruelty that manifests itself in violence and the systematic oppression of those who do not conform to a society's concept of "normal."

In the West, "normal" largely means Caucasian, Christian, straight, and male. I tick all but one of those boxes, which is why, as I type these words, I'm actually aware of the whiteness of my fingertips. How many times have I been subject to injustice? None. When have I been on the receiving end of systematic oppression? Never. Do I exercise prejudice against others? Yes—all humans do, to a greater or lesser extent, no matter their religion, education, gender, and race. We might, for reasons of preconditioning or personal experience, just not like the look of someone's face. We might, for whatever reason, just not like the sound of their voice. And, I suppose, that is the tricky truth of the matter: What divides us is not the fact that we are aware of our differences, but how we respond to that awareness. While we might not be able to extinguish prejudice altogether, it is very possible to end inequality, injustice, and marginalization, to make our differences the cause of celebration, not division. That, I believe, is the underlying desire that motivates the photographers in this section.

Drawing on personal experiences and the experiences of others, these photographers expose and challenge injustices relating to sexuality, race, gender, faith, and disability. While they and their subjects have been forced to endure tragedy, oppression, and violence, the work does not attempt to assign blame or ask for your sympathy. Rather, the photographers respond to our divisive world with unwavering strength, compassion, and even humor. Here, the beauty and potency of visual language is the weapon of choice with which to educate others.

When looking at work like this—work that exposes the inhumane side of human nature—it's nice, or somewhat reassuring, to believe in the unifying power of art, to have faith that it can make a positive difference. But it's not art's responsibility to change anything. That responsibility lies on the shoulders of those who view it, who connect with it, who are moved enough to acknowledge and take action against the latent cruelty within us all.

SION

Here, the beauty and potency of visual language is the weapon of choice with which to educate others.

Who, if anyone, is able to be themselves?

The question is, who are these men? Clearly, they do not want to be pictured: at least, they do not want their faces to be. But what is also clear is that these are not stolen snapshots of strangers. The images feel posed; it feels as if the men, to a certain degree, are collaborating with the photographer. These portraits come from Laurence Rasti's series There Are No Homosexuals in Iran, a title borrowed from a statement made by former Iranian prime minister Mahmoud Ahmadinejad. Having been forced to flee Iran, where homosexuality is punishable by death, the individuals in Rasti's photographs currently reside in Denizli, a Turkish town that has become a haven for those seeking asylum in more sexually tolerant countries in the West.

Rasti pictures these men at home, in nature, and during matrimonial celebrations, their faces often obscured, their identities unknown. Sometimes there is a clear interaction taking place between photographer and subject; couples pose under patterned blankets, behind flowers, and among balloons. In other seemingly candid moments, the mood is cautious, a little unforthcoming, and it's unclear whether the body language between men is affectionate or confrontational. This very apparent tension between public and private, self-expression and self-consciousness, speaks to the state of limbo, both psychological and geographic, that these men have been forced to endure. The dynamic between the photographer and her subjects, one that plays with intimacy and distance, gives us an insight into a protected world of forbidden love and desire, a world that is acutely vulnerable to the incrimination of the direct gaze of outsiders.

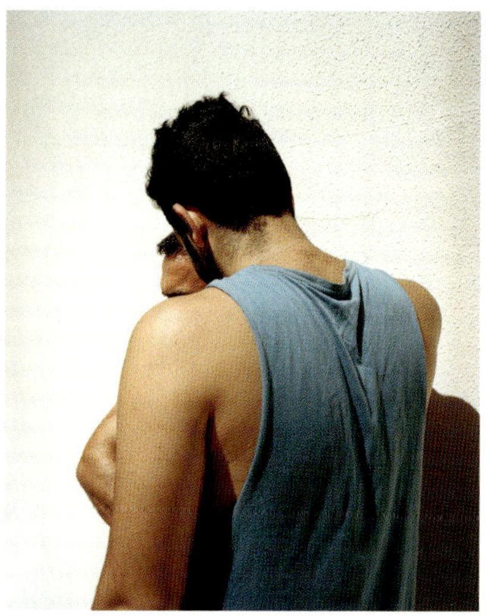
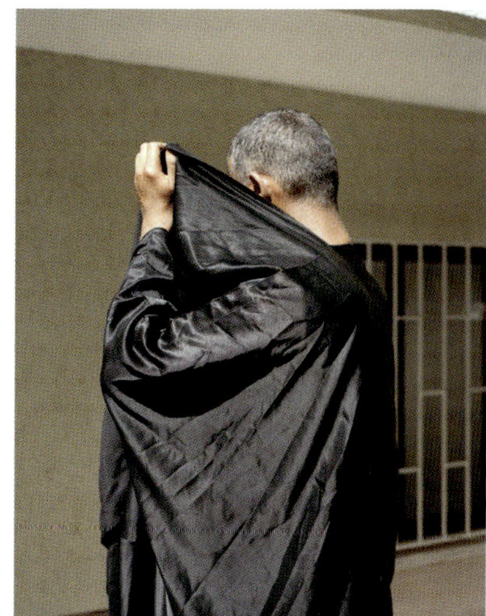
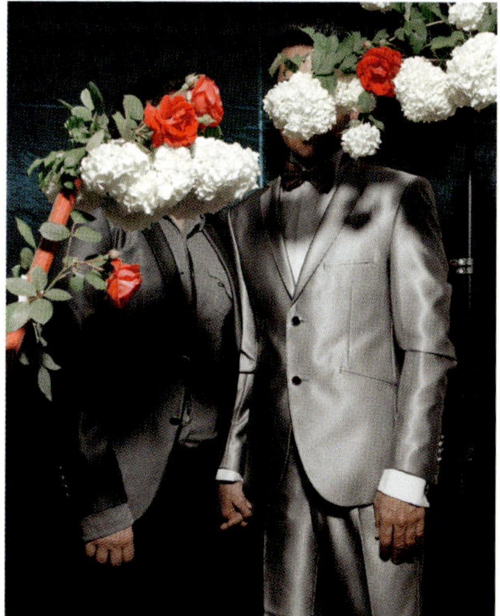
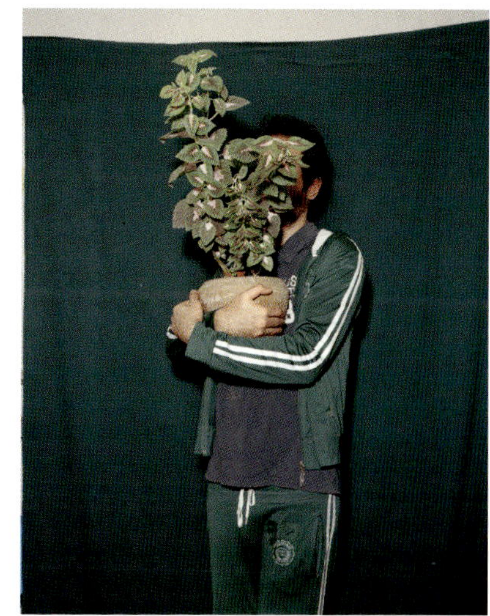

Photos from the series There Are No Homosexuals in Iran, 2014-16

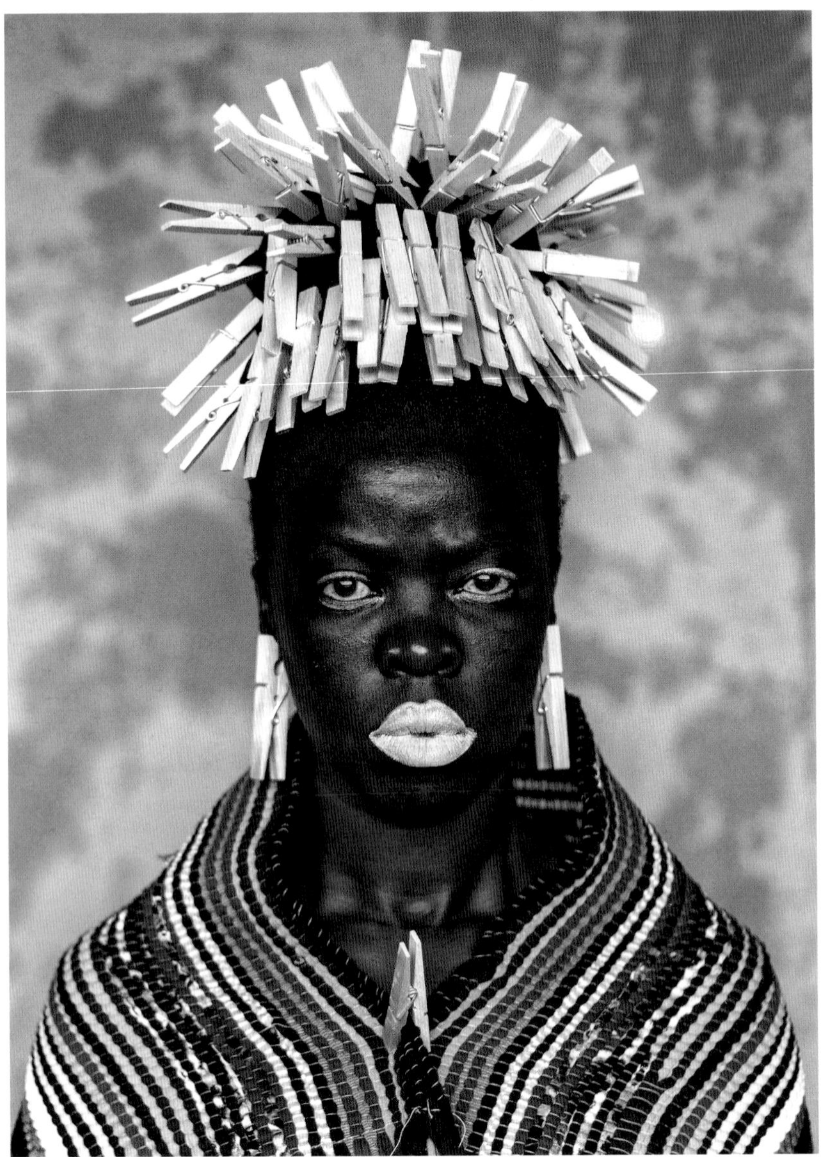

Bester I, Mayotte, 2015

For the "visual activist" Zanele Muholi, the camera is a weapon—one she wields against the long-established history of hatred and violence against South Africa's Black LGBTQ community. Defiant, confrontational, disdainful, vulnerable—pick your adjective while

When you look at a portrait, do you feel seen?

staring into Muholi's unblinking eyes, which confront us in this series of self-portraits titled Somnyama Ngonyama (Zulu: "hail the dark lioness"). Adorned with domestic objects such as clothes pegs, electrical cables, inner tubes, and vacuum cleaner pipes, Muholi dismantles the conventions of photography's history, one that has monotonously depicted individuals of other cultures, especially those in Africa, as mysterious creatures, primitive and wild in their elaborate tribal garb. But for Muholi, who is part of the LGBTQ community, these self-portraits extend beyond the reclaiming of Black identity. They serve as a defiant, unashamed proclamation of personal beauty and self-empowerment. In fact, Muholi consciously enhances features by making skin appear darker, eyes bright, and lips occasionally defined by white. The directness of the gaze manages, somehow, to nullify the humor or absurdity of the costumes, making it impossible not to feel targeted, accountable, when looking at the portraits. The camera is, indeed, a weapon and by pointing it inward, Muholi is drawing a slow and steady bead on you.

Does
change
have to
come
from
above?

The skies across America were pretty serene on May 30, 2020, when the words fluttered overhead. The streets, however, were not. Following the death of George Floyd, who died under the suffocating knee of a police officer in the U.S. Midwestern city of Minneapolis, people of all colors defied curfews to protest the injustice. Neighborhoods became tinderboxes of fury, chaos, and uncertainty, and the world, once again, waited and watched for a single spark that would ignite the entire nation.

Jammie Holmes, however, went about expressing his rage through very different means. He hired planes to fly over New York, Los Angeles, and other major cities, pulling banners that quoted the last words of Black people killed while in police custody—phrases such as THEY'RE GOING TO KILL ME, PLEASE I CAN'T BREATHE, and EVERYTHING HURTS. Such language took on new resonance when isolated in the sky and immortalized in images. In many images taken by members of the public, the plane, as if instinctively, was cropped, making the words appear to have been spoken by a higher power.

At the risk of picking apart a work so conceptually crisp, it's worth reflecting on why Holmes's protest became one of the most enduring visual responses to George Floyd's death. The answer lies in an accumulation of creative contrasts. Firstly, there is the primed canvas of blue and white; one could not have wished for a more hopeful sky on which to place these violent words. Secondly, Holmes co-opted planes that usually pull marriage proposals, happy-hour offers, and other declarations of celebration and affluence, to deliver a message almost unthinkably grave. And thirdly, during a time of such tragedy and unrest, the silence and separation of Holmes's protest managed to rise above the noise, literally and metaphorically, giving voice to those who could no longer speak.

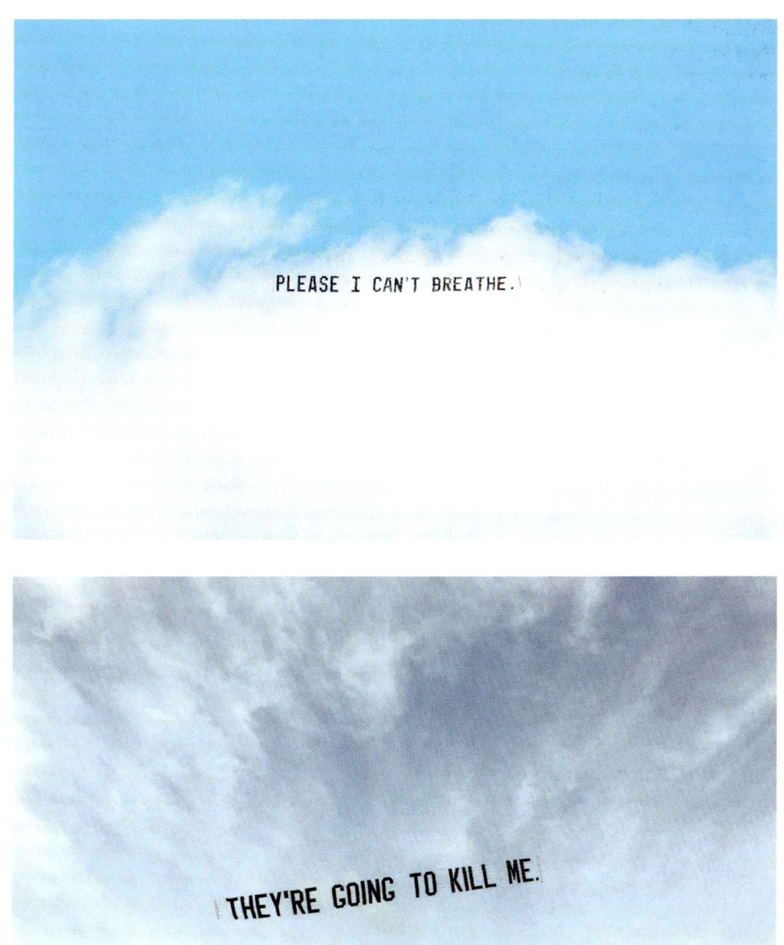

Top: *Please I Can't Breathe*, 2020 | Bottom: *They're Going To Kill Me*, 2020

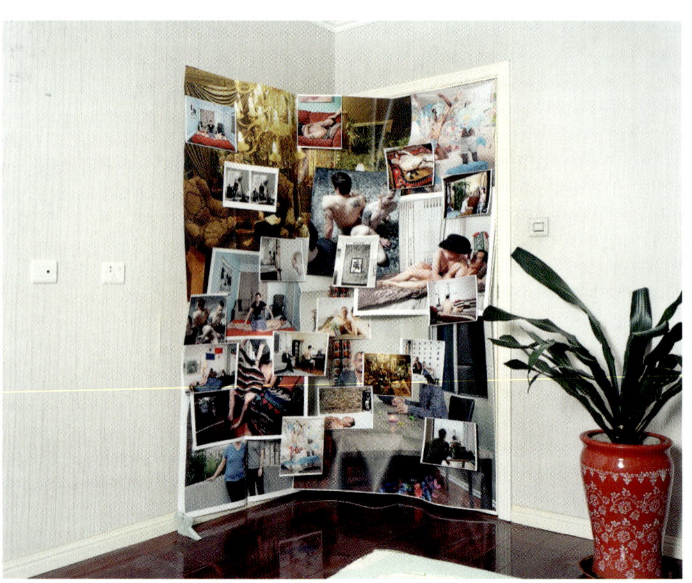

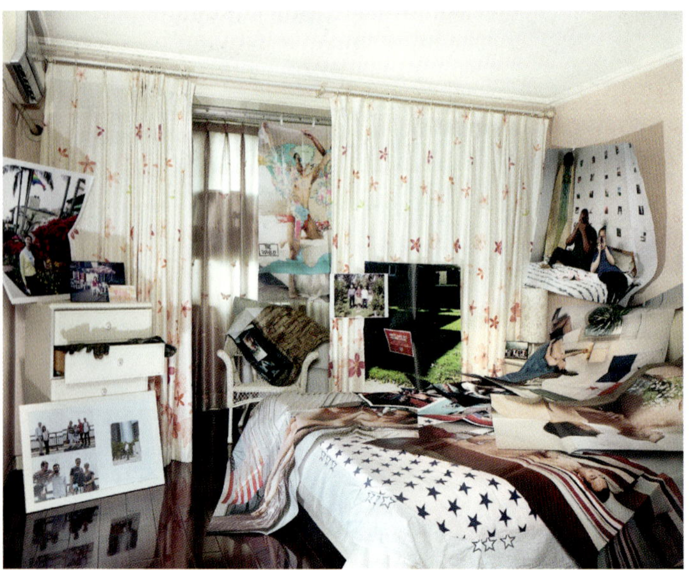

Top: *Behind My Door*, 2018 | Bottom: *Parents' Bedroom*, 2018
Following spread: *Worlds Within Worlds*, 2019

It was a remarkable act of teenage rebellion, executed by a fully grown man. When the U.S.-based artist Guanyu Xu visited his parents in Beijing, he waited for them to leave for work and then plastered his photographs all over their very traditional home. Portraits of him posing with male lovers, cutouts of homoerotic heroes from American pop culture, and other, more global references to political and cultural divisions filled drawers, were draped over his parents' bed, and exploded across the dining room. Xu photographed his completed installations and then returned everything to normal before his parents came home.

Imagine: When they opened the door, everything was exactly as they left it, including their son, who in their eyes remained a straight man whose artistic endeavors extended no further than innocuous photos of landscapes. Xu's desecration of his parent's home, the same home in which he'd lived as a teenager, was a way for him to reclaim the space where his sexual identity was formed and to challenge China's condemnation of LGBTQ communities as well as the conservative views of his father, a military man. Xu's imagery and his expressive arrangements completely disrupt the normalcy of a neat and tidy home, with its floral patterns and impeccably made beds. His visual mixology transforms politically correct rooms into spaces that celebrate individual freedoms and challenge nationalistic governance; the home becomes super-charged, an amalgamation of differences that find a way to coexist.

Do your parents know who you are?

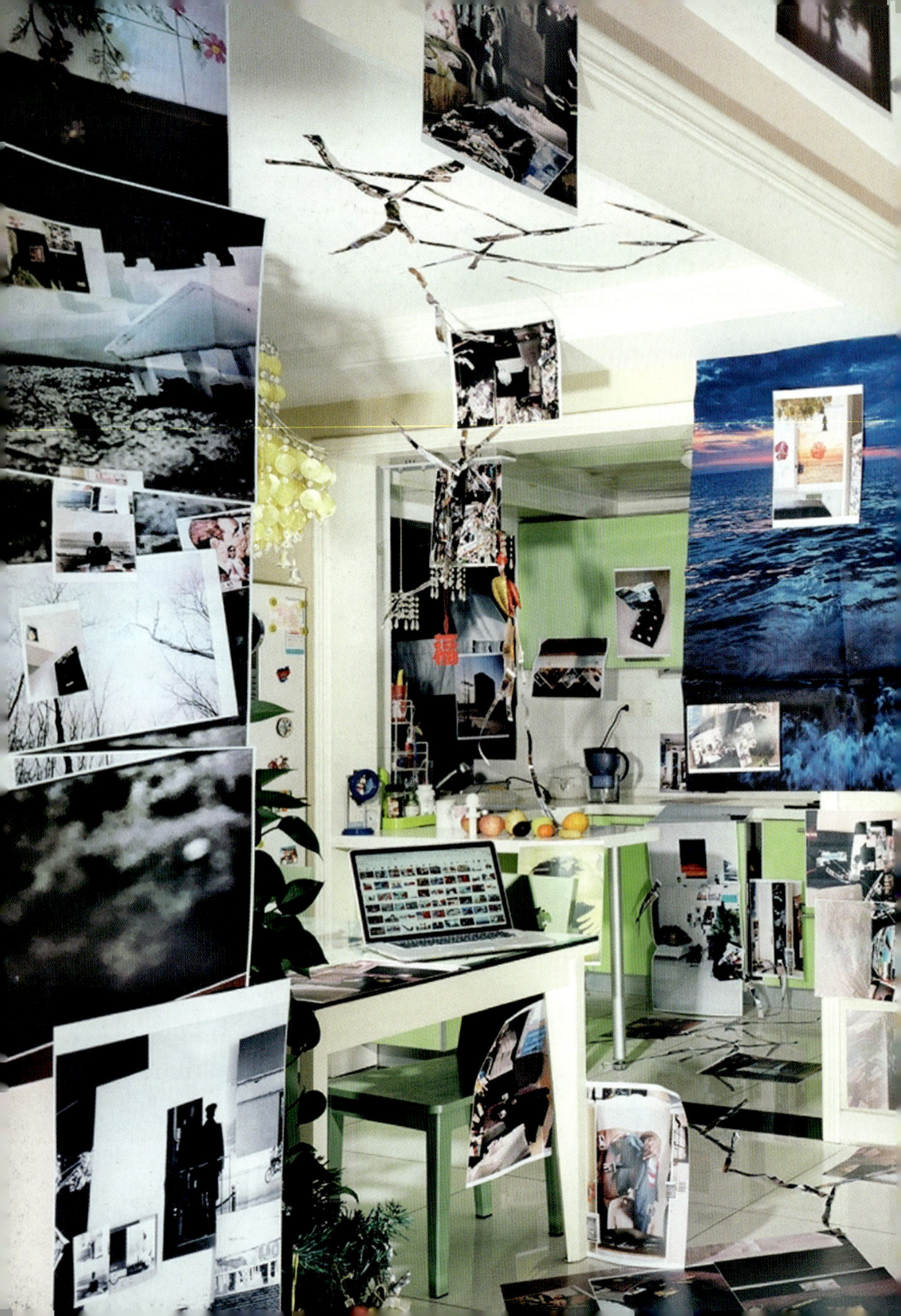

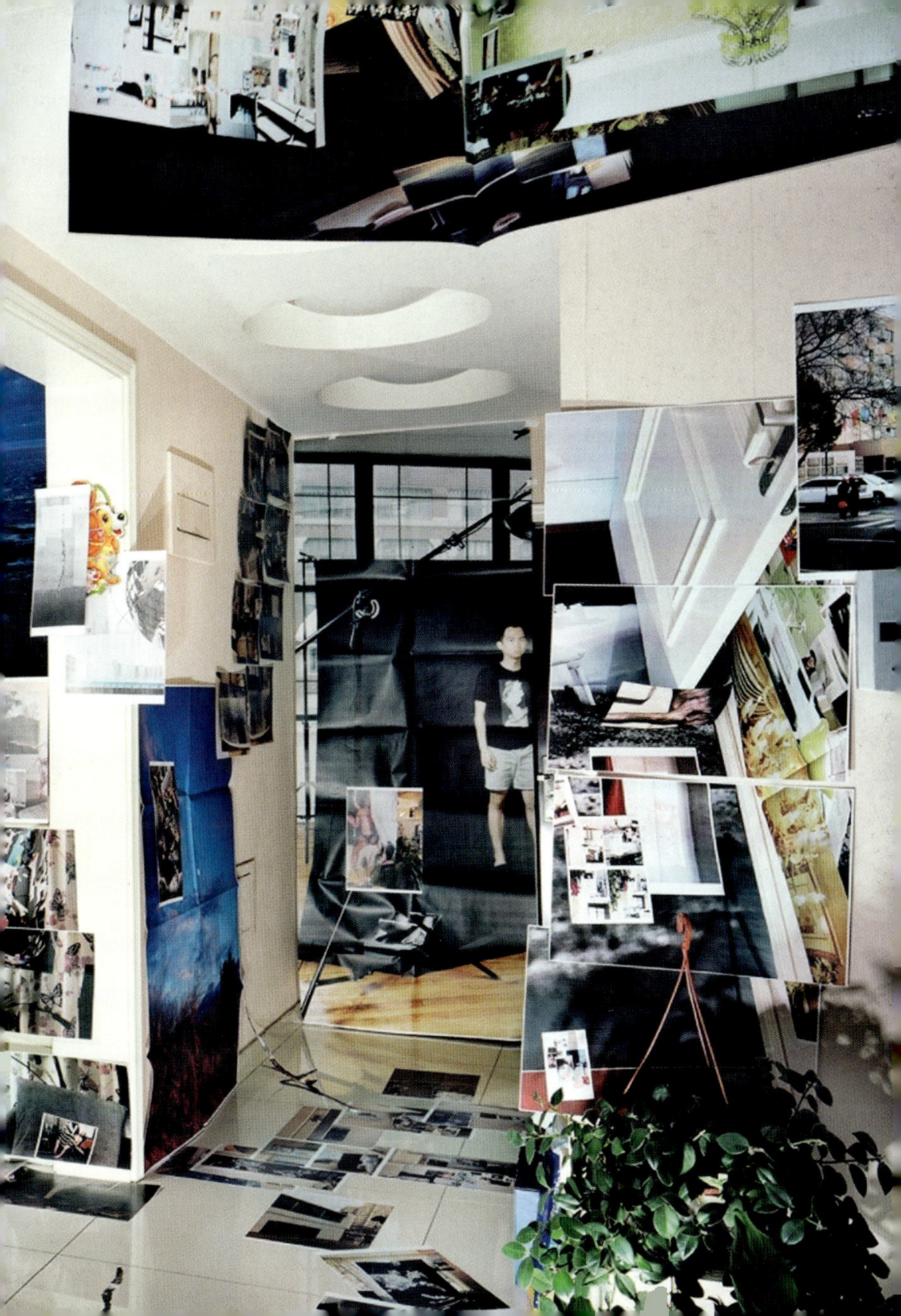

We cannot see the woman's face, but we can feel her stare. Against the flame-like rocks, and in opposition to the flamboyance of the billowing red dress, her posture is casual, a touch nonchalant. The image, by the photographer Keyezua, is the culmination of a long creative process in response to family trauma, disability, grief, and the inequality of women in her home country of Angola. Before his death, Keyezua's father fell ill and lost both his legs.

Do you see people with disabilities as weak?

Over time, her grief and frustration grew into a defiant visual language that hits back at the prejudicial attitudes that Angolan society holds toward those with disabilities, and in particular the emasculation of men without legs.

The imposing mask worn by the woman in the image was made by a group of men who had also lost their legs due to illness. The creation of the mask was an opportunity for Keyezua to reconnect with her lost father by spending time with those who had endured similar psychological upheavals that resulted from having their role and social standing stripped away for reasons beyond their control. The men made six masks in total that are worn by Keyezua's model in other images. In each image there is a palpable sense of resilience, even anger, that offers an alternative visual approach to representing disability. Rather than a suggestion of victimhood or weakness, what we have here is an all-encompassing declaration of strength. The mask is a charged object that confronts rather than conceals, almost like armor, and the formidable presence of the model is certainly not to be messed with.

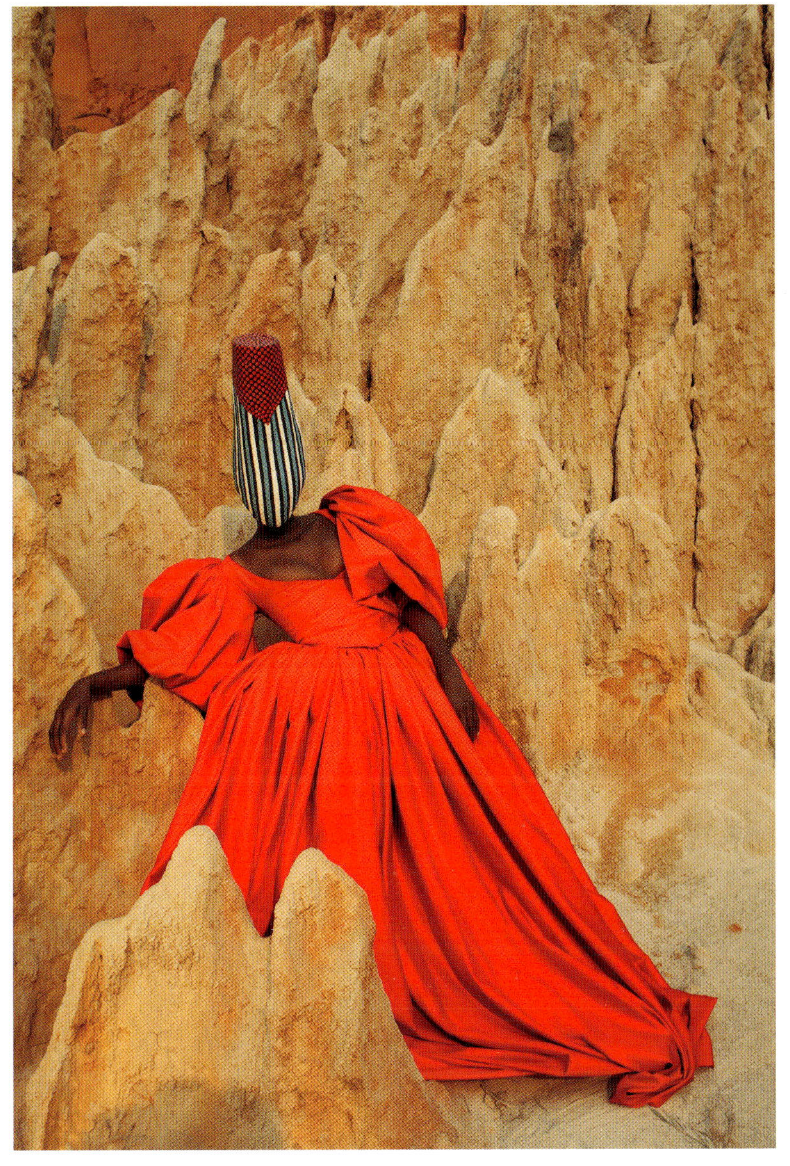

Fortia 01, 2017

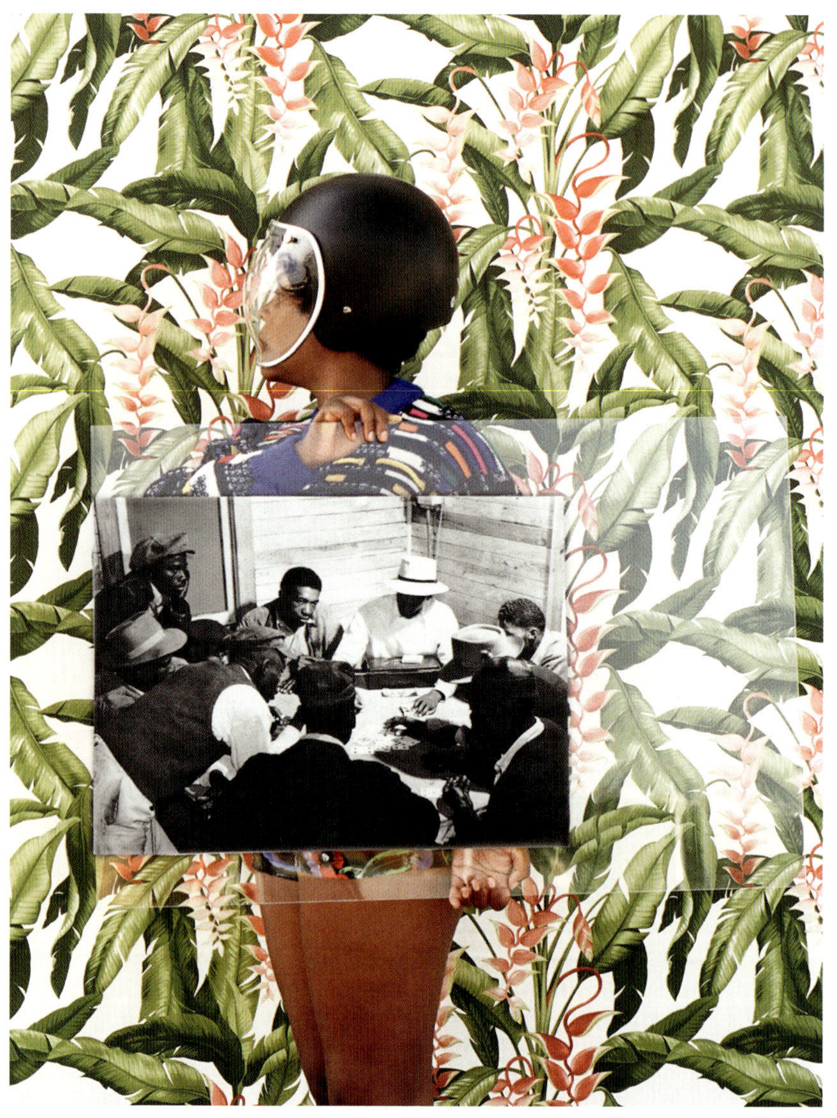

Sundown (Number Six), 2018

Xaviera Simmons picks away at accepted histories that still serve as the foundations of white supremacy in the United States. This image, titled *Sundown (Number Six),* takes its name from "sundown towns," communities of the Jim Crow era, a time when laws were in place that enforced racial segregation, where Black Americans were not welcome after dark. Drawing on imagery and motifs

What are you shielding yourself from?

associated with this time, Simmons photographs herself against a floral backdrop while wearing a police riot helmet and holding a black-and-white photograph taken in 1941 by Marion Post Wolcott. The photograph shows a huddle of African-American men inside a Florida juke joint. Such places served as safe places for Black Americans to gather in areas where they were barred from openly congregating. This monochrome window into the past contrasts with the vibrancy of the backdrop, confronting us with past truths as well as acting like a shield, but what is it defending Simmons against? The innate suppression of the white gaze? Memories of a violent history that built a nation by exploiting and abusing African-American slaves? The all-too-common aggression targeted at Black Americans today? All of the above, most likely. By layering references to established social systems of suppression, Simmons denies us the ability to conveniently forget a shameful history. She literally holds it up to her audience, an audience made up of people who have benefited from, and been persecuted by, what they are seeing.

**RYAN
DEBOLSKI**

Do you really believe all people should be equal?

Without context, these men could be asylum seekers, washed up on a distant shore, awaiting acceptance in a country far from home. Yet the beach is the only place they can escape to. These men, these workers, are not welcome in the luxurious air-conditioned plazas and palaces that their hands build in the desert heat. Ryan Debolski's series LIKE centers on Indian men who have left their families behind in order to earn a living as laborers in the wealthy country of Oman. Photographs of bricks, diggers, concrete rubble, and other details from construction sites sit alongside pictures of the men at play, their bodies glistening in the sun, their clothes soaked in seawater, and their limbs interlocked in boisterousness. This piecing together of images, set in the nondescript context of the beach, creates a portrait of dislocation. The men appear out of place, untethered to their surroundings, and the building materials seem abstract, without purpose.

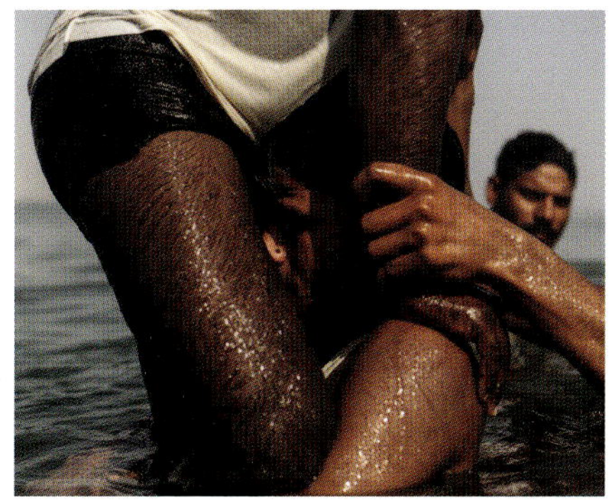

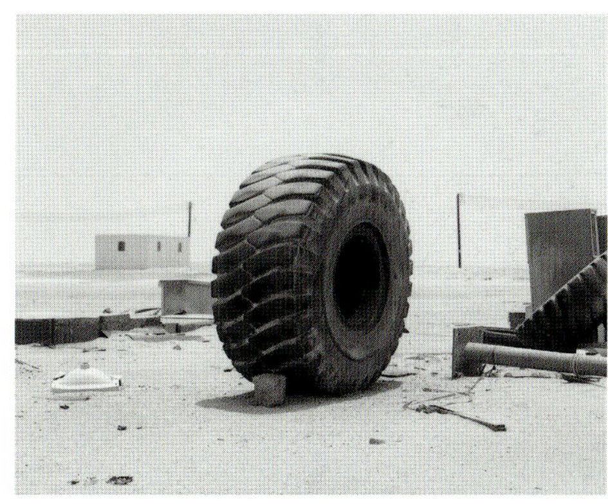

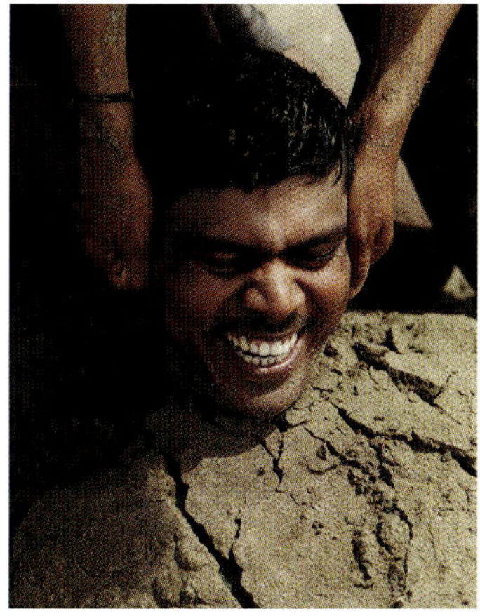

Above and following spread: Photos from the series LIKE, 2020

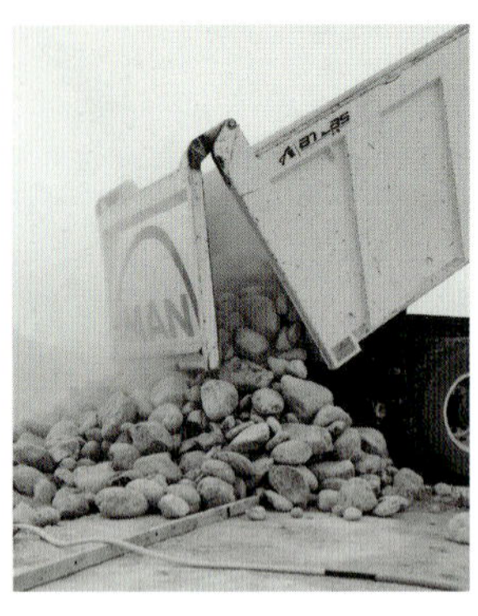

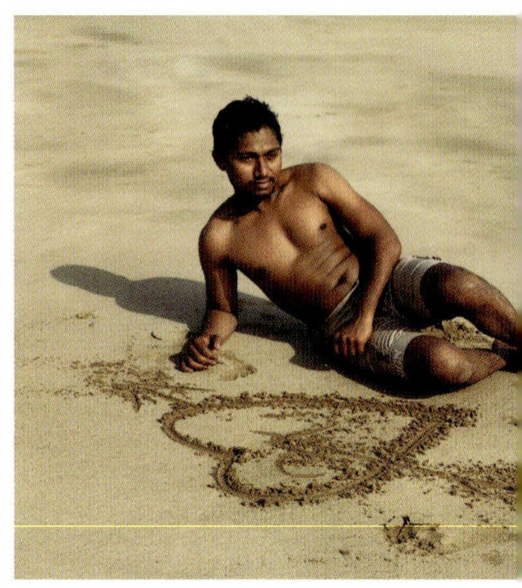

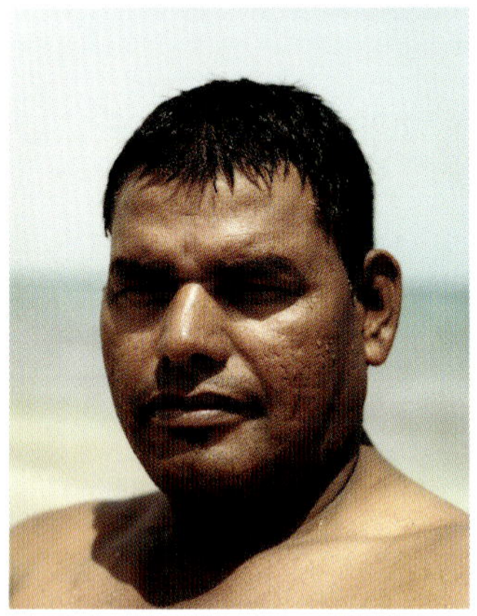

At no point do we see a finished building: everything is in progress, nothing is settled or complete. Debolski's mixing of black-and-white and color photographs sets up a constant exchange between present and past, hope and melancholy, moments to be remembered and forgotten. Humanity and warmth are felt in his pictures of men innocently interacting on the beach, yet his tight compositions suggest confinement, and the bare, sandy bodies start to feel like a metaphor for these

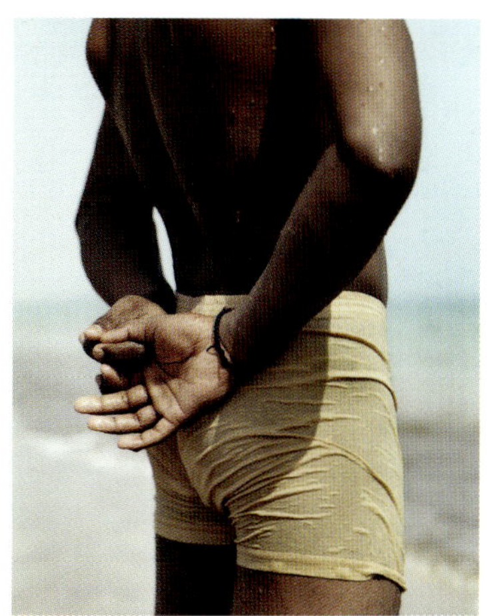

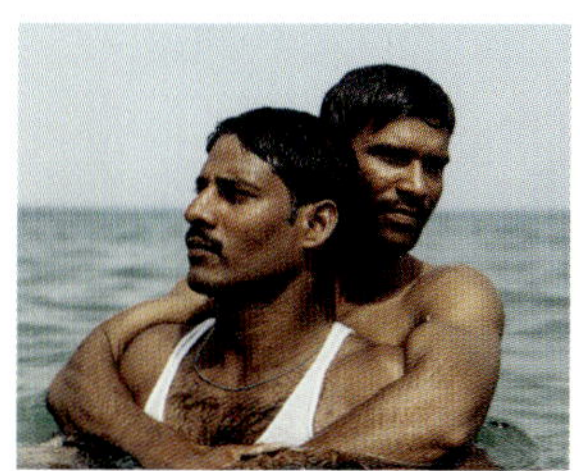

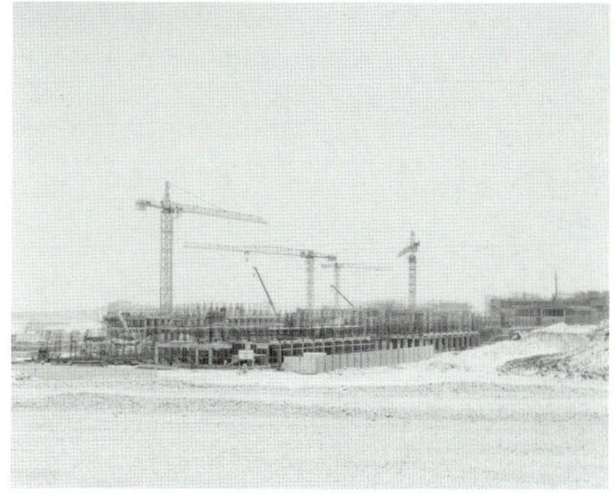

workers' position in the grand scheme of things. They are
trapped in a globalized system that forces them to remain
at the bottom; their hands and bodies continue to build the
glass towers for the world's richest. With tenderness and
respect, Debolski shows us the faces of very modern slaves
in a very modern world. He provides insight into men whose
only security is one another, whose only taste of freedom is a
narrow sliver of beach.

"With that little camera he sucked a sad poem right out of America," wrote Jack Kerouac about Robert Frank's series The Americans. Sixty years later, and Kerouac's beating prose applies just as well to Doug Rickard's photographs that form *A New American Picture*. Using Google Street View, Rickard clicked his way through the forgotten communities of the United States, sliding down dilapidated streets, past derelict homes, abandoned cars, and anonymous strangers. He didn't have to leave his house, but make no mistake, Rickard is a street photographer. During his excursions, he would occasionally pause, look closer, and take a picture of the screen, digitally erasing any of Google's iconography to free the image from its original context. The resulting photographs depict telling details, caught unconsciously by Google's automated camera, that paint an isolating portrait of the forgotten.

Is there intention behind every image?

Gravity seems to have a harder pull on the people and places in Rickard's pictures. In one photograph, a lone Black man stands beneath a wall and the painted words above him reading "Super Fair" become stained with sad irony. By rephotographing this scene, one originally captured by the lens of such a wealthy company, Rickard draws our attention to an apparent moment of "nothingness" that exposes the gaping divide between those with and without power. In another image, a family tends to their front garden. There is a touch of bleakness to the scene, but also beauty, as each of the individuals could not be more perfectly positioned in the composition. From one image to the next, you can't help wondering why such a powerful corporation is so obsessively photographing the most powerless communities. Do we live in a world where images hold more value than the people within them?

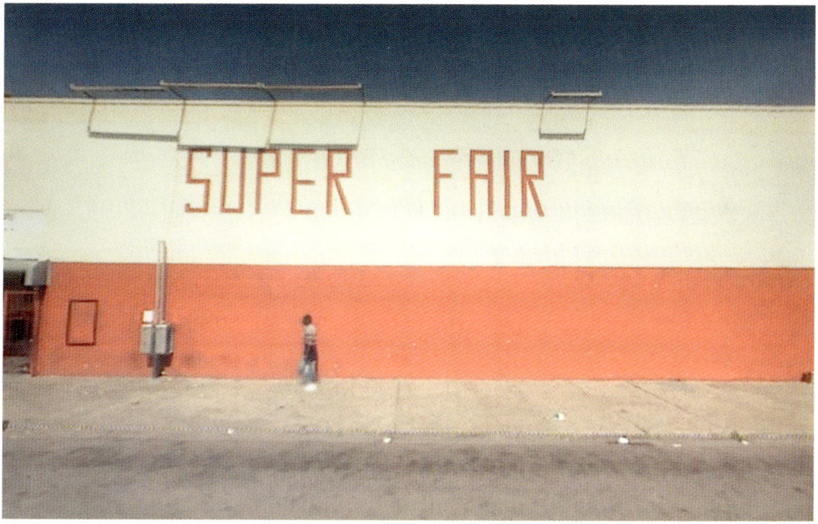

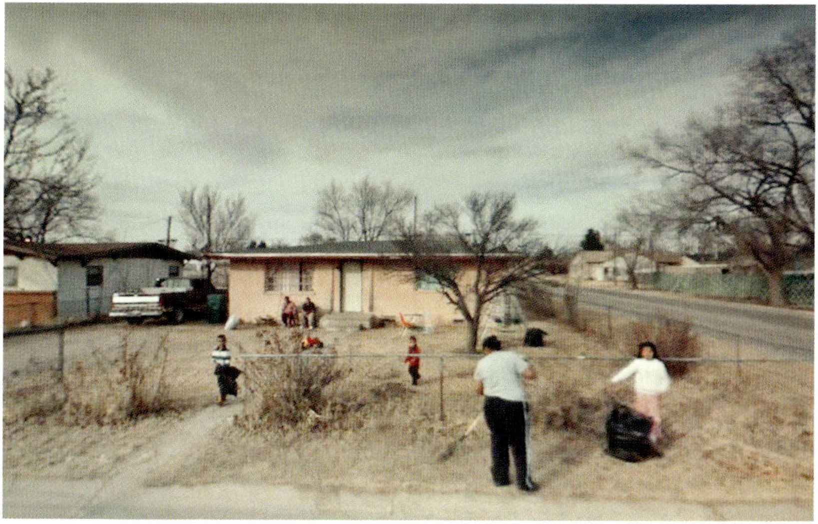

Top: #41.779976, Chicago, IL (2007), 2010 | Bottom: #104.573110, Lovington, NM. 2008, 2009

I have two Instagram accounts. One is my personal account, the other belongs to Darrell and Patricia, my right-wing alter egos. I often check in to Darrell and Patricia's feed to see what information bubble is forming around them. There's a lot of gun-toting Trump talk, claims of election fraud, and anti-Muslim memes, but there are also open displays of love for community and family that, I have to admit, warm my heart at times. When I created Darrell and Patricia, I didn't think all that much about who they were. I had a fairly one-dimensional idea about what outside influences might be shaping their values and beliefs. But now, after a year of living with them through COVID-19, BLM protests, and the 2020 U.S. election, they feel more real, more like fully formed humans. This isn't because Darrell and Patricia are particularly active on social media—they mostly post pictures of their Rottweilers. It's because, in my mind, they have become shaped by what surrounds them, the information that the platform wants them to see and information regurgitated by the people they follow. This amounts to specific messages, mostly promoting fear, that have filtered down to Darrell and Patricia from the higher powers of government and multibillion-dollar corporations. And as much as our political and social views are misaligned, I am quite fond and forgiving of D&P, because they, like you and I, are not in complete control of what they think.

The work
is intended
not
as a
call to arms
but
rather as
a call to
awareness.

Social media is one example of mind control, and it does little to hide its algorithmic techniques of influence. As the photographers show here, the real world—that is, the physical world—is governed by just this kind of systemic structure of control. Their work looks at the influence of education, work life, advertising, surveillance, incarceration, and rebellion in order to reflect on why we believe as we do, behave as we do, and tolerate what we do. Talk of unseen "systems" at play can often come across as paranoia, but the photographers here respond to very apparent, very obvious societal structures—structures so entrenched, so much a part of who we are, that they often go unchallenged or unnoticed. These structures are systemic and intangible; their presence is more mental than physical, but they might as well be the walls of a maze, built and reinforced by human hands over millennia. The work discussed in the following pages is intended not as a call to arms but rather as a call to awareness.

Governments and tech companies now have the ability to manipulate our minds and control our movements to an unprecedented degree of precision, and our only means of resistance is to form a deeper understanding of who we are and why. As for D&P, they don't stand a chance. After all, they are completely unaware of their puppet master, the entity that controls everything they post. Then again, who is pulling my strings?

LINDSAY GODIN

Do school children need to be lied to?

Nationalistic messages, both overt and covert, adorn the walls in Lindsay Godin's photographs of classrooms. On the painted cinder blocks hang posters and slogans espousing military might as a force of good, the triumphs of the Founding Fathers, the American flag as a symbol of belonging. These messages are often pictured coming from the mouths of bygone movie stars such as John Wane, Sylvester Stallone, and Marylin Monroe, who are, themselves, as ingrained in American national identity as George Washington or Abraham Lincoln. Imagery of Native Americans serves as another key component of American history. These figures appear proud and strong in their headdresses, a people celebrated rather than exterminated. Some scenes are not without their quirks. In one image, Godin places us in the position of teacher, looking out toward a classroom in which the feet of the desks are covered by tennis balls. This detail might be humorous if it wasn't for the bold red and white stripes painted across the ceiling. Under that banner, one senses the presence of an authoritarian figure with an intolerance for marks on the floor, let alone opposition to the American Way.

Godin has made no attempt to hide the institutional aspect of the rooms themselves. She photographs them as they are, often without any natural light and under the glare of fluorescent tubes. Strip away the posters and these rooms could form the architecture of any military base or correctional facility. Godin's clinical and empty classrooms, absent students and their raucousness, give us a space to reflect on how the ideologies of adults were shaped as children. The graduates of these rooms may go on to become leaders of business and politics, yet their relationship to the world, what underlies their ambitions, their career trajectories, and sense of self, was written on the walls of their childhood.

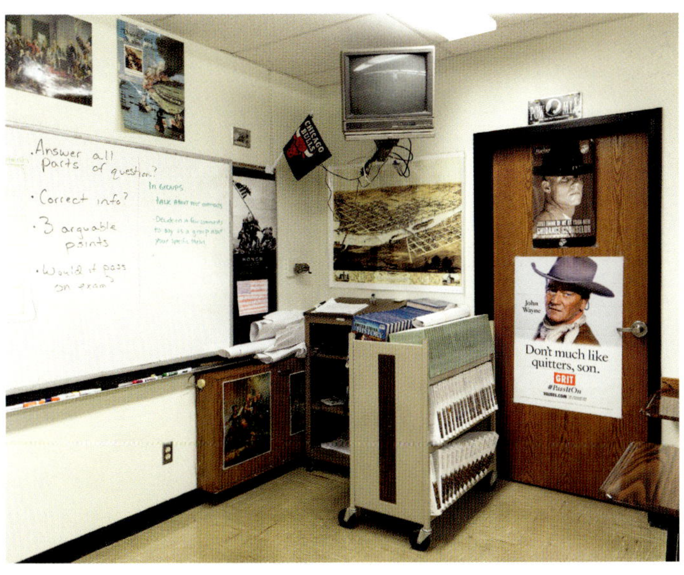

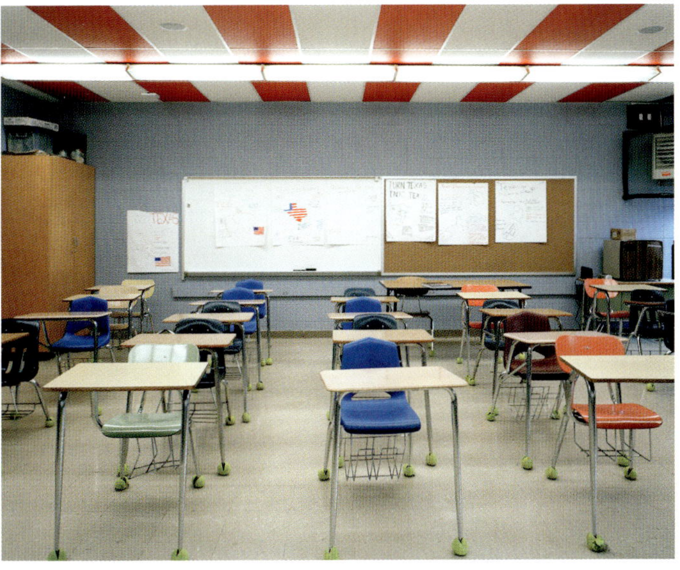

Top: *Don't Much Like Quitters*, 2016 | Bottom: *Turn Texas into Texus*, 2016

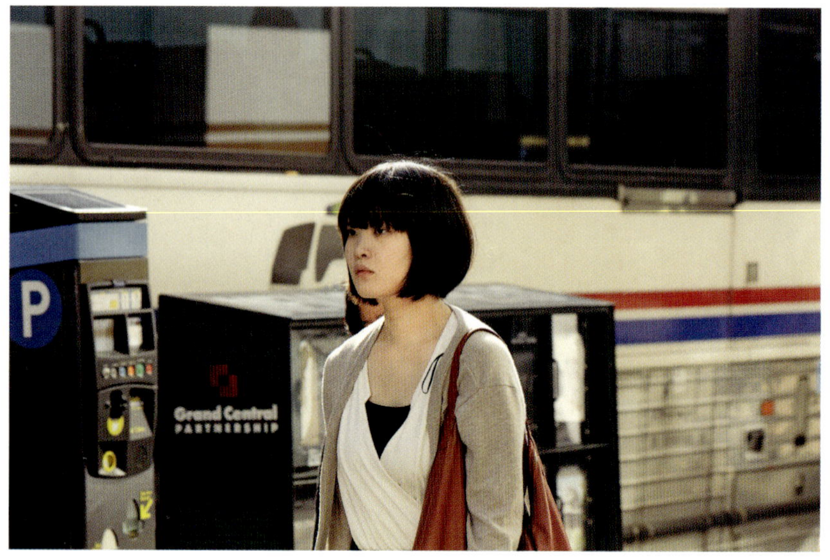

2012.06.08 08:25:58

Who is,

in fact,

the boss

of you?

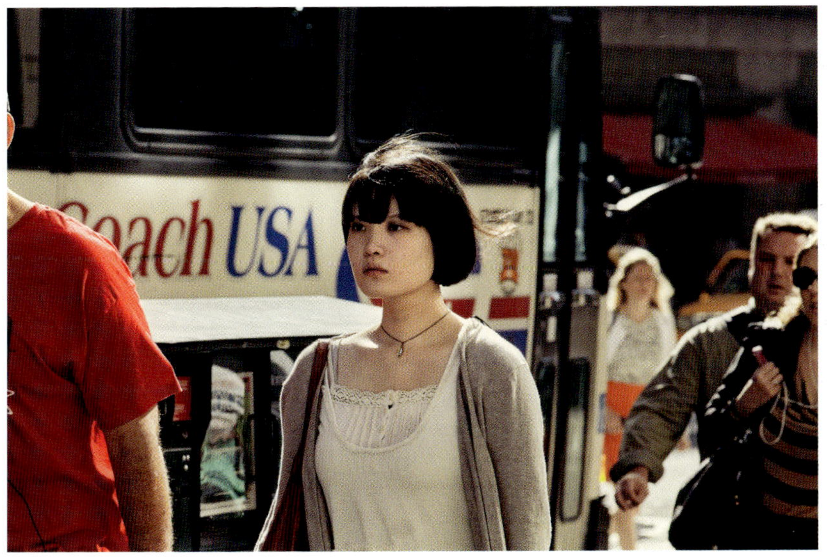

2012.06.27 08:33:09

A young woman gazes fixedly ahead as she walks down the street, the sunlight drawing a silver line around her gray cardigan and reflecting off her hair. And there she is again, same fixed gaze, same cardigan, same light. At first it seems like these two photographs were taken moments apart, but then we notice her shirt is different, her bag on the other shoulder, her hair slightly longer. All of a sudden, the unseen time between images multiplies, seconds into minutes, minutes into weeks, weeks into months. It must be street-photographer's luck, we assume, that brought this woman in front of Peter Funch's lens not once, but twice.

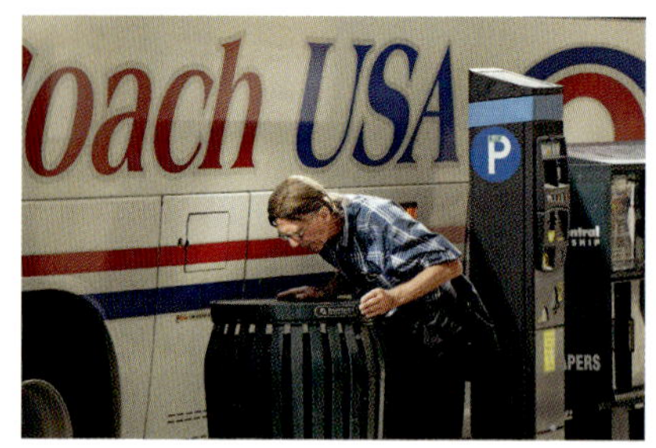

2012.07.18 09:16:02

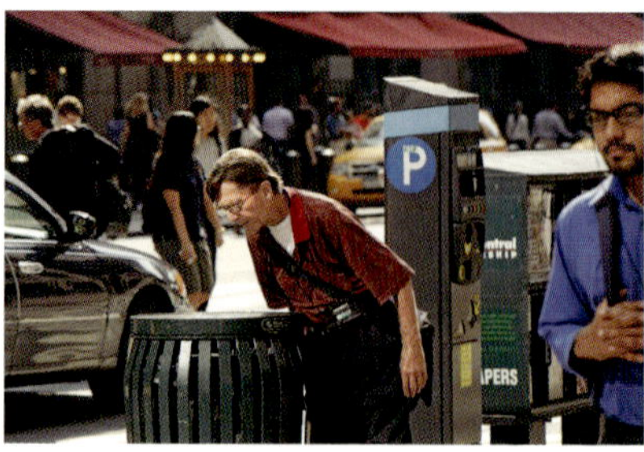

2012.07.23 09:15:20

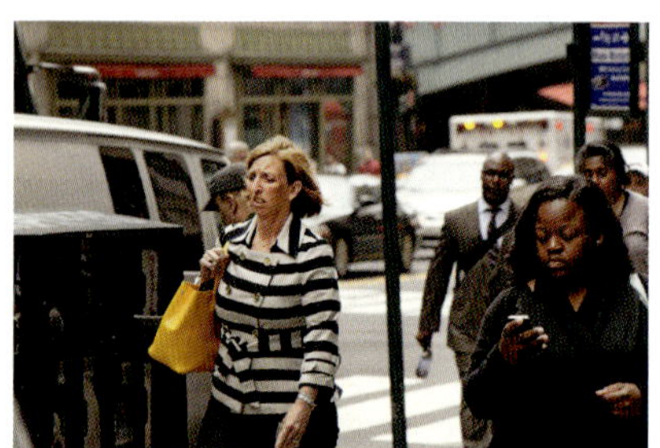

2012.06.27 08:33:09

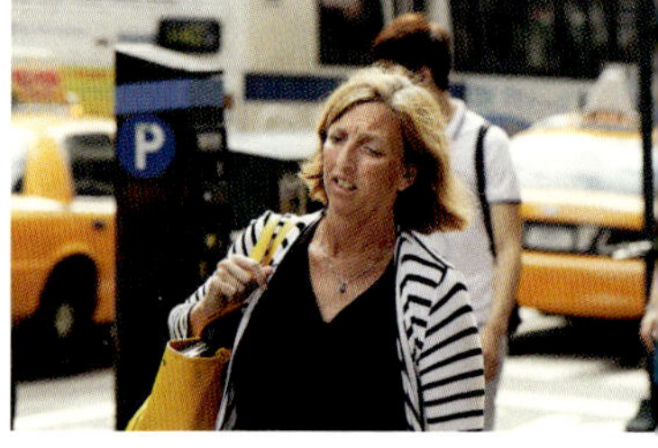

2013.06.14 08:41:41

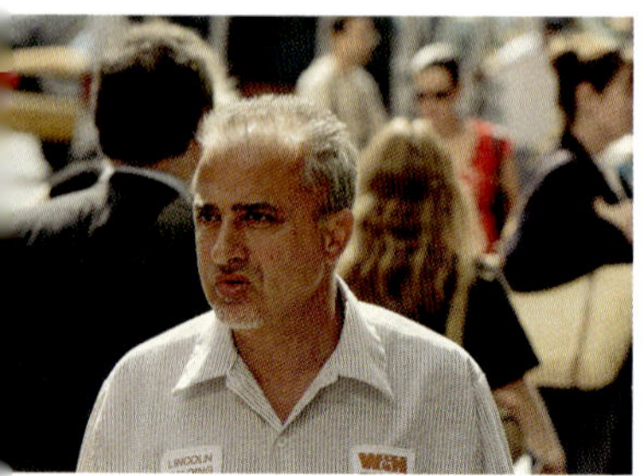

2007.06.28 08:59:39

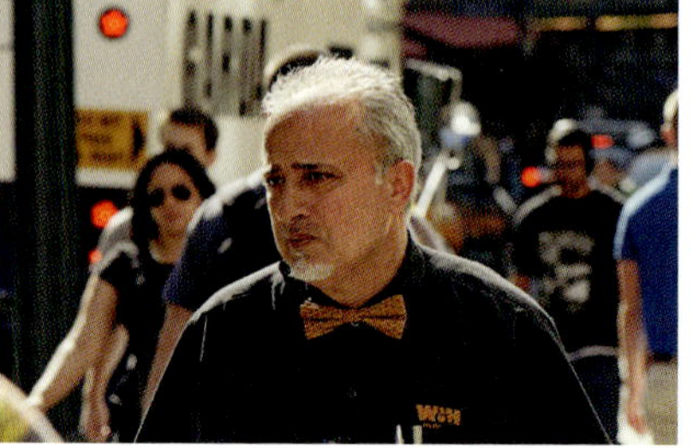

2012.07.03 08:54:01

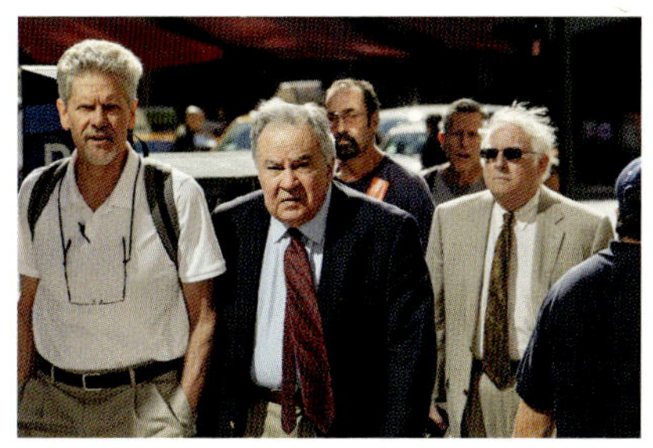 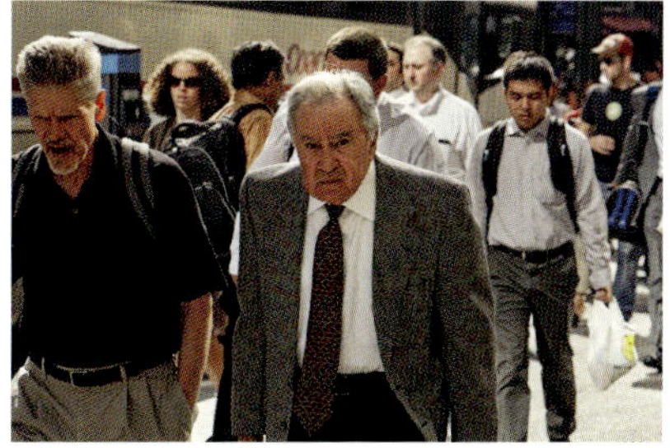

2012.06.27 09:16:42   2012.07.10 09:21:20

2012.06.27 09:16:42

2012.07.10 09:21:20

However, when we look at his images, taken from 2016 to 2017 between 8:30 A.M. and 9:30 A.M., of people walking by East 42nd Street and Vanderbilt Avenue, a nondescript corner of Midtown Manhattan, a pattern emerges. People, mostly commuters, show up again and again, day after day, in the same place at the same time. Even their clothing—something we tend to regard as an expression of freedom and individuality—varies only slightly, if at all, from one image to the next. The startling revelation in Funch's photographs is not that we are creatures of routine—we all know and live that—but the extent to which the people depicted, though physically "there," appear mentally absent. Like almost all of us, their movements and choices are controlled without them even knowing, controlled by their work, the expectations of others, a need to belong. Yet they are people, with diverse lives. Photography asks us to fixate on the moment captured, but here, Funch draws our attention to what might have occurred to the subjects between pictures. Did the subject fall in love? Did the test results come back negative? Was someone born, did someone die, and did the subject, for whatever reason, pick something different from the lunch menu? Whatever might have taken place, nothing has trounced the invisible systems at play that keep these people returning, as if in a trance, to the same spot, at the same time, over and over again.

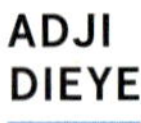

Are you what you eat?

Adji Dieye turned her attention to bouillon cubes, in particular the Maggi cube, in order to expose the complicated relationship between branding, visual language, and cultural identity. In the late nineteenth century, the Western "scramble for Africa" saw countries divide Africa into manageable zones with which to form trade agreements so that large corporations could flood the continent with foreign-made products and brands. Using collage, and referencing poses similar to those seen in the studio photography of Malick Sidibé and Seydou Keita, Dieye's images at first appear to conform to what the global art market has come to demand from West African artists—vibrancy and playfulness. Yet here, Dieye has weaponized these visual conventions.

Two Senegalese women are dressed in robes that match Maggi's brand colors. If it weren't for the masks covering the women's faces, they might appear to be proud brand ambassadors as they stand over the cubes. The oversize cubes themselves sit on the ground as if they are the building blocks of Senegalese cultural history. However, these cornerstones of the kitchen were originally created and imported from Europe, their popularity fueled by their persistent visual presence on billboards and supermarket shelves throughout Senegal. For Dieye, these half-inch cubes of vegetable and meat flavorings are far from innocuous. She sees them as conveniently packaged morsels infused with the kind of colonial insidiousness that millions of people ingest, quite literally, every single day.

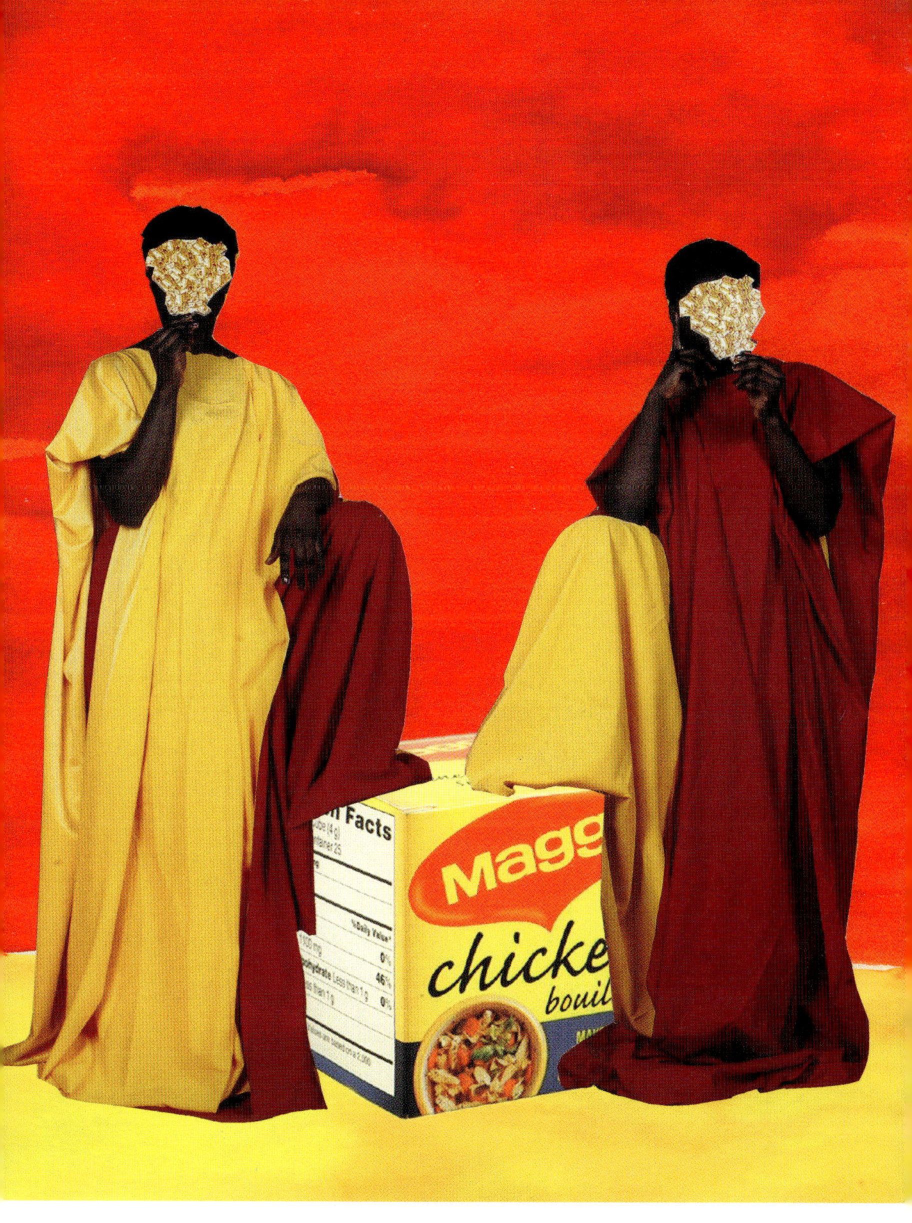

Maggic Cube, Gagnez Un, 2019

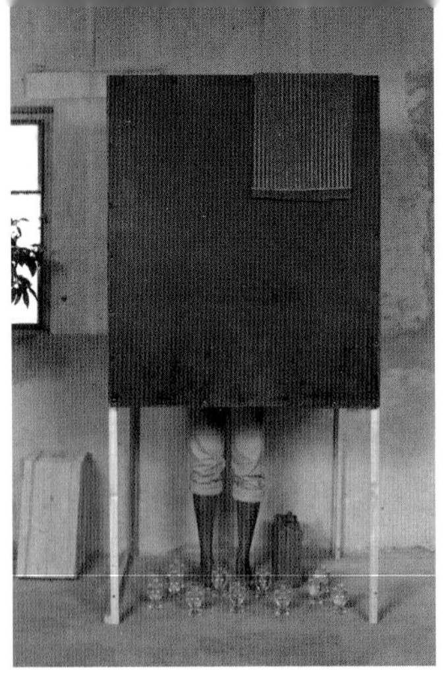

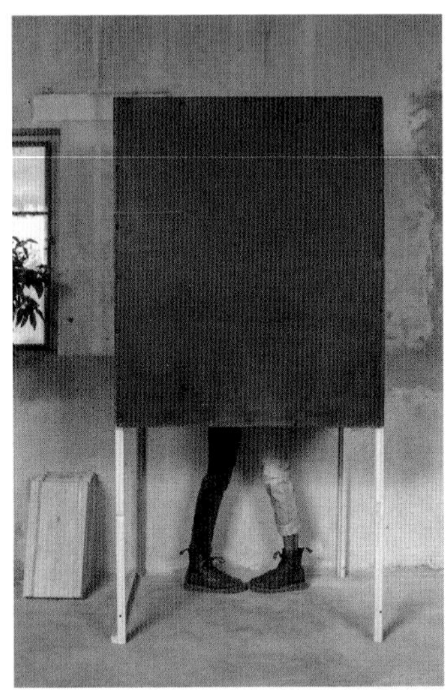

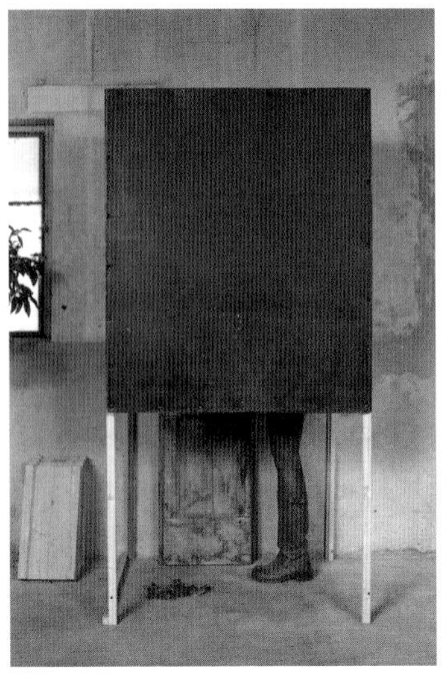

Photos from the series Election Box, 2012

What is happening here? Who do these legs belong to, and what are they doing inside this box? And what is the box? Some kind of rudimentary photobooth perhaps, or a changing room? It is, in fact, an election box, at least, a re-creation of one made by, and containing, Silvia Rosi. While working as an election clerk in Italy, Rosi observed people casting their votes and was struck by the absence of Black bodies inside the boxes. As someone who was born and raised in Italy, and the daughter of Togolese migrants, Rosi knows all too well how hard it is for those of African descent to become citizens of a country that does not recognize "jus soli," a system granting automatic citizenship to those born in a country. Instead, Italy favors bloodlines when it comes to granting citizenship, and those who do not fall into the right category must enter a relentless bureaucratic process to prove their longstanding permanent residency.

In making and occupying her own election box, Rosi assumes a state of anonymity. With just her legs visible, her body comes to represent all the Black bodies that cannot contribute to Italy's electoral process. In images pointed yet playful, we see Rosi act out various facets of herself, whether memories, dreams, or fantasies, but nothing is explained. It seems that the artist feels no obligation to share the truth that is revealed inside a box that is, of course, intended to provide the occupant with the privacy to express themselves in order to have a say, to have control on the society to which they belong. The tension between being on the outside and being on the inside is palpable in Rosi's photographs. We, the audience, are the ones being denied access. The box becomes mysterious and sacred, a safe space providing security and refuge to those on the inside, and an impenetrable barrier to everyone else.

Who decides who decides?

Is social order more fragile than we think?

Look again at Rodrigo Valenzuela's photograph and you will see that all is not what it seems. In the foreground, the objects exist in three dimensions, but as we travel further into the image, what we initially perceived as a continuation of space is an illusion, nothing more than an image of the same objects taped to the wall. A clever visual trick, indeed, but what, for Valenzuela, is the significance of these items? While he was growing up in Chile under the dictatorship of Augusto Pinochet, tires, cinder blocks, folding chairs, sheets of corrugated metal, and wooden benches became the building blocks of barricades, erected by citizens in order to protect themselves during protests from the authoritarian government, a phenomenon we have seen more recently in protests in Hong Kong, the United States, and other seemingly settled societies. Working in the studio, Valenzuela elevates these rudimentary objects into symbols of defiance. He builds barricade-like structures and photographs them. He then makes large prints of the images, hangs them behind the structures, and rephotographs the scene, occasionally altering the position of objects.

This visual strategy of construction and deconstruction presents disorienting layers of reality that are, at first glance, intentionally confusing. Metaphorical mirages, as it were, that demand a closer look. At times his scenes resemble makeshift zoo enclosures, with little swings and climbing frames set against the illusion of space; a suggestion of captivity, perhaps. In shifting our perceptions of familiar objects, Valenzuela shows that nothing remains the same. Leaders rise and fall, socialism flips to capitalism, capitalism to socialism, and in the process, wheels become weapons, benches become barricades. When it comes to defending one's freedom, the meaning of everything and anything is up for grabs.

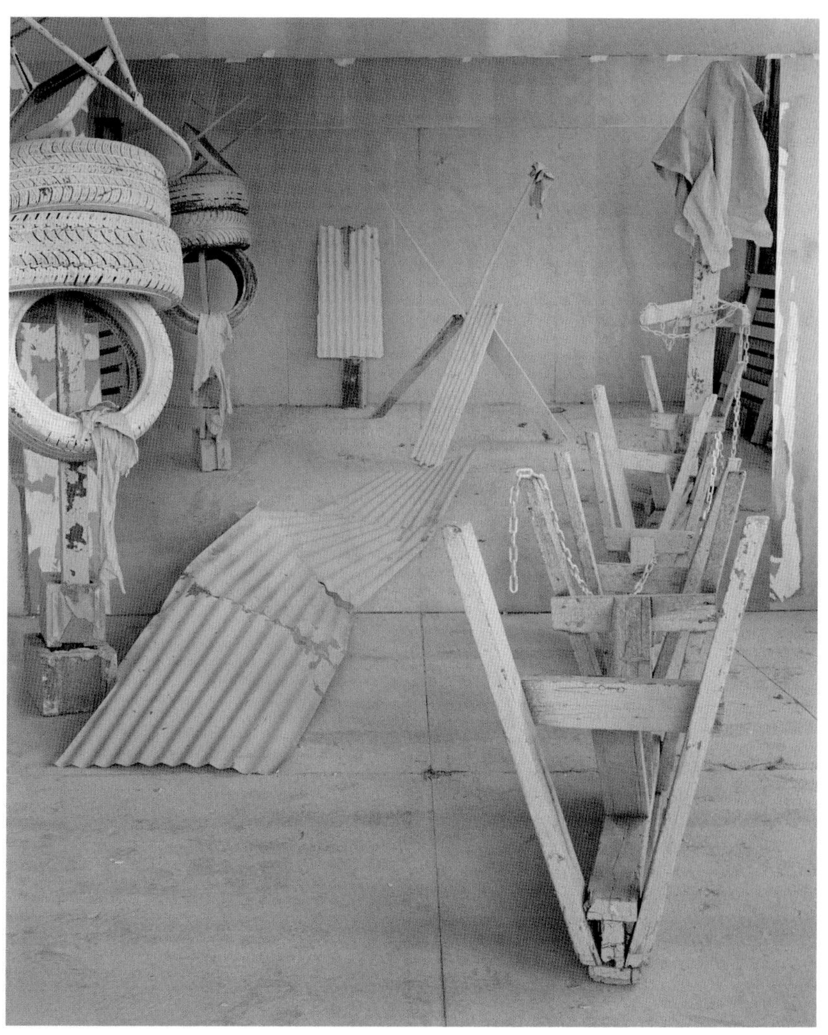

Barricade No. 2, 2017

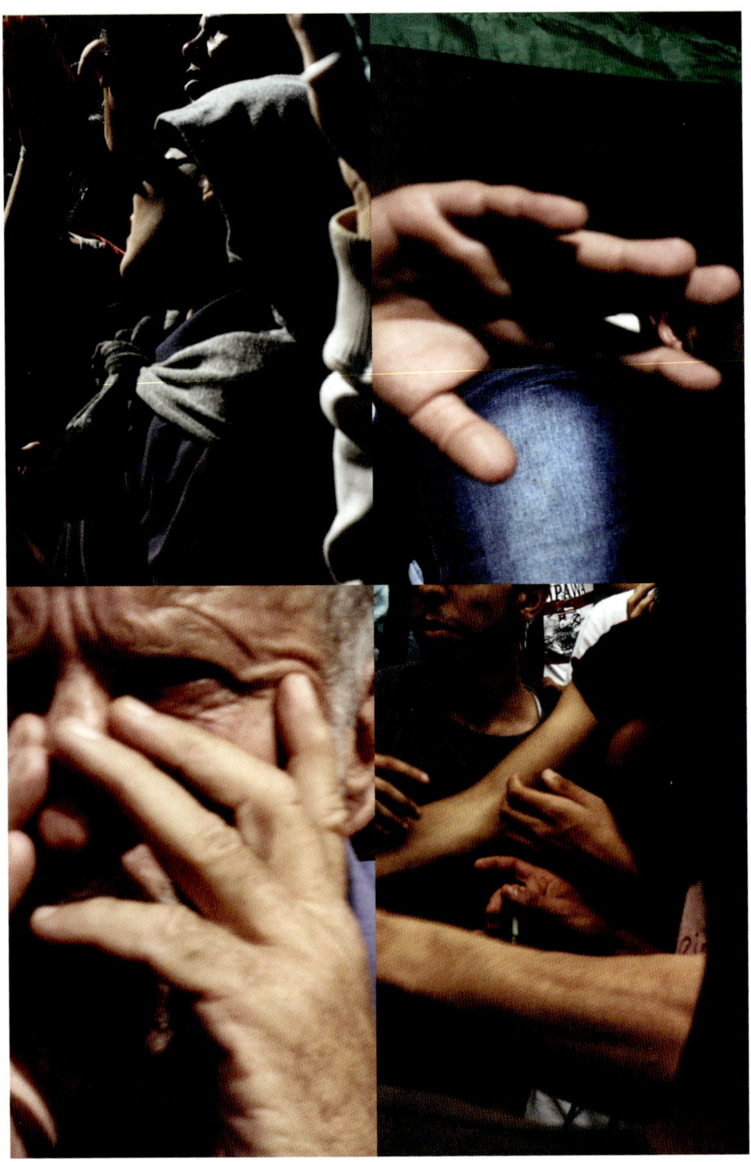

Photos from the series A Little Louder, 2019

Does protesting give you a greater or lesser sense of self?

With tightly cropped photographs of protestors, Abdo Shanan offers us an intimate yet charged perspective of demonstrations in Algeria. Protesting has not, in recent years, been commonplace for Algerians—one of the last major demonstrations, in 1988, was shut down by the government with such brutal force that it resulted in the deaths of more than five hundred people. The demonstrations depicted in this series erupted in early 2019 in response to the ongoing and corrupt rule of President Abdelaziz Bouteflika. Shanan threw himself into the thick of it.

Close-ups of chanting faces, young and old, fill his images; arms, hands, light, and shadow dissect compositions. Small details and gestures become emotionally charged: the way a man's fingers wrinkle the skin on his forehead, the sunlight interacting with a passing hand, the gentle, slightly concerned way in which one person clings to another. And when seen together, the individual images form a larger picture of the protests that edges toward abstract expressionism. In opposition to media images that deindividualize protesters by fixating on the size of the crowds, here we see a tense ecosystem of individuals, each with their own values and emotions. We become aware of the discrete uniqueness of "protesters" who are usually thought of as identical atoms that simply add up to one unified mass. Shanan shows us that "a protest" is tens, hundreds, thousands, or in this case millions of individual protests. He suggests that when so many strangers gather in order to defend their freedom, the power of their protest lies not in what they share but in where they differ.

**CLÉMENT
LAMBELET**

Could a computer ever predict your behavior?

Seven facial expressions, thought Charles Darwin, are universal. That is to say, all human societies, no matter where they are situated or how isolated they might be, will recognize when someone looks angry, disgusted, contemptuous, happy, sad, fearful, or surprised. Hardly surprising, then, that software companies have exploited this hardwired human characteristic in the form of facial recognition software to analyze how we might feel and behave based on our expressions. Concerned by the ever-increasing use of such software on social media and in public spaces, Clément Lambelet went about conducting an experiment. Using as his starting point a library of low-resolution images of actors performing these universal expressions, Lambelet cropped each frame tightly around the face and then ran the image through a widely used algorithm developed by Microsoft. He then presented everything in a photobook titled *Happiness Is the Only True Emotion*—because, as it turned out, the only expression the algorithm could read with total accuracy was happiness. All the others were frequently miscategorized.

This fearful face, for example, was read as being surprised. Flicking through Lambelet's playful series quickly becomes a

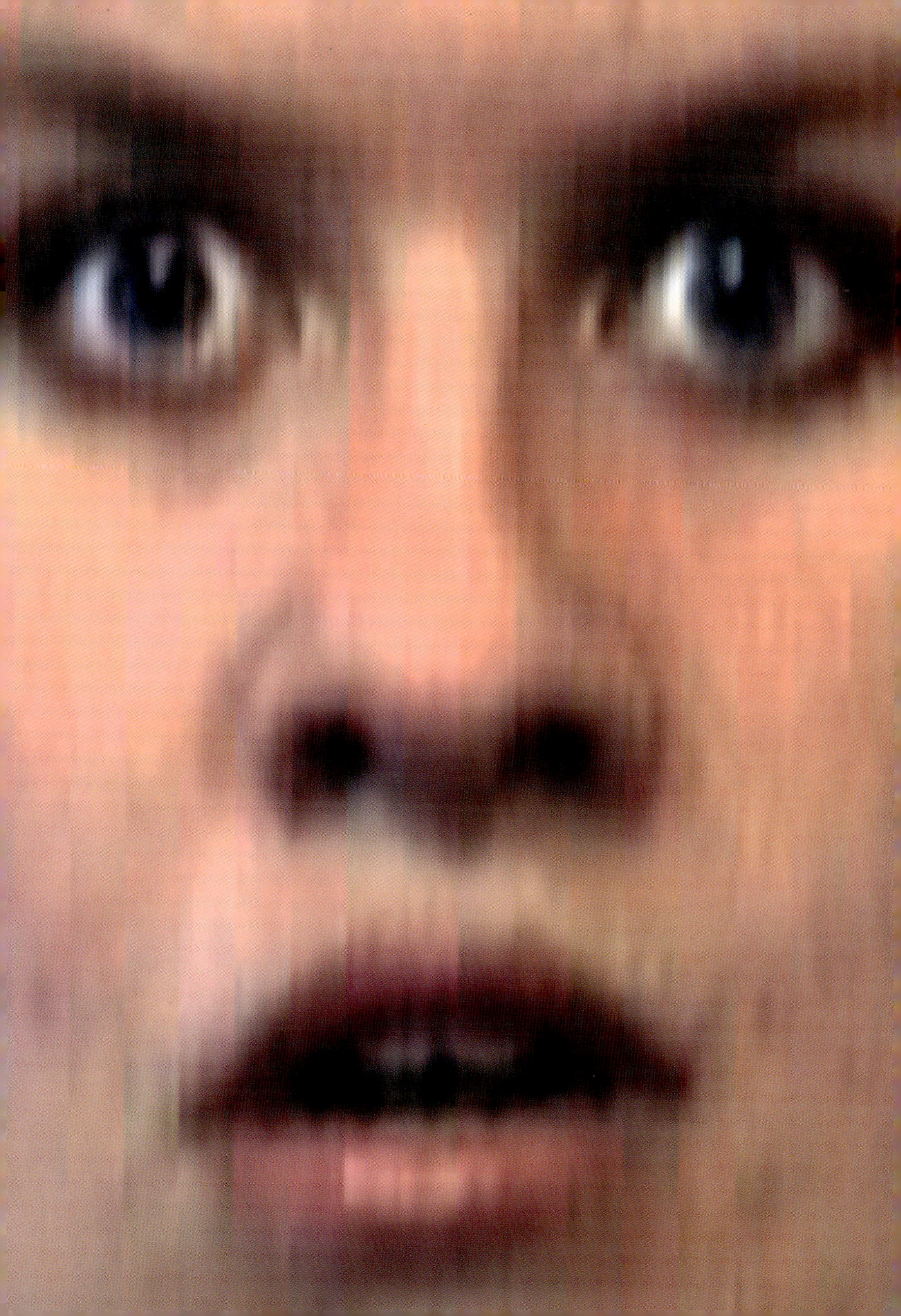

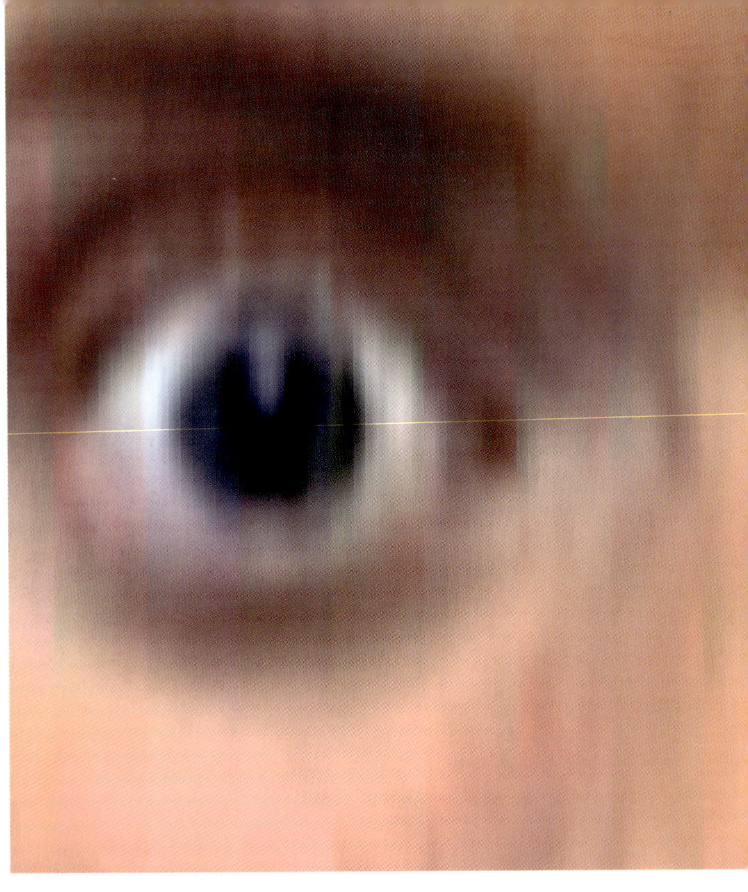

more disturbing exercise. Not only does it undermine technology's ability to understand people, it strips us, too, of an innate skill that Darwin argued should come naturally. The tightly cropped images remove the faces from context, even from the bodies to which they belong. They become abstract, digitized surfaces made up of specific components that prompt us to become as coldly analytical as a computer. In a strange way, we are able to "empathize" with the computer's inability to feel its limitations when it comes to understanding people.

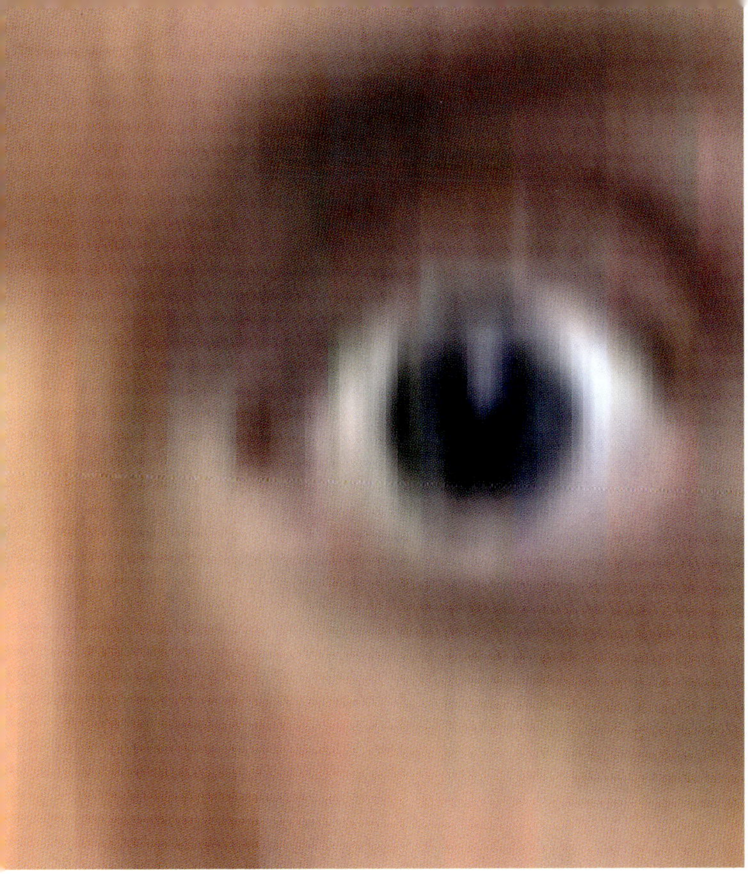

Lambelet's library of expressions reminds us how precious and highly developed real-life human-to-human interaction is. How it is based on much more than simply the way someone looks. More than that, his work brings to the surface something really quite worrying: When it comes to social order, when it comes to deciding who does and does not pose a threat, relying on such rudimentary technology is a little like asking an infant to make the decisions for us. And just like an infant, this technology does not, as yet, have any real understanding of the human mind.

Previous page: *f8f1.jpg (fear)*, from *Happiness Is the Only True Emotion*, 2019
Above: *f4s1.jpg (surprise)*, detail, from *Happiness Is the Only True Emotion*, 2019

Above: *17/35 (Not the Man I Once Was)*, 2009–16
Following spread: *Nine Years out of a Death Row Sentence (Forest)*, 2009–16

When does incarceration become torture?

For several years, Amy Elkins exchanged letters with men sentenced to life or death in prisons across the United States, most of whom were in some form of long-term solitary confinement. Over the course of her correspondence, Elkins gained a deeper understanding of what life was like for these men, including the psychological implications of such strictly enforced isolation. The men shared distant memories of childhood, dreams of the outside, and dying wishes. In response, Elkins pixelated portraits of her pen pals using an image-loss ratio based on the number of years each man had spent behind bars to the number of years they had been alive.

In the resulting images, the men are visible but obscured, the algorithm creates a separation between us and them. In other works, Elkins uses appropriated images to create composite landscapes based on memories shared in these letter exchanges. The number of layers in each final image equals the number of years served by each prisoner. In one of these composited landscapes, we see a forest. The spellbinding light makes it feel enchanted, like a place of magic and possibility, while the layers of murky vegetation add density and darkness accompanied by a sense of foreboding.

Elkins's process of removal, of visual and emotional distancing, goes beyond the question of an individual's guilt or innocence to reflect on the systematic erasure of these men from recognition, from memory, and from society. How does long-term isolation affect one's mind, connection to the past, perception of time passing, and sense of existence? These hazy images, where men appear like ghosts and where landscapes are no more tangible than dreams, ask at what point punishment ebbs into torture. We can take away someone's freedom, but what claim do we have on their soul?

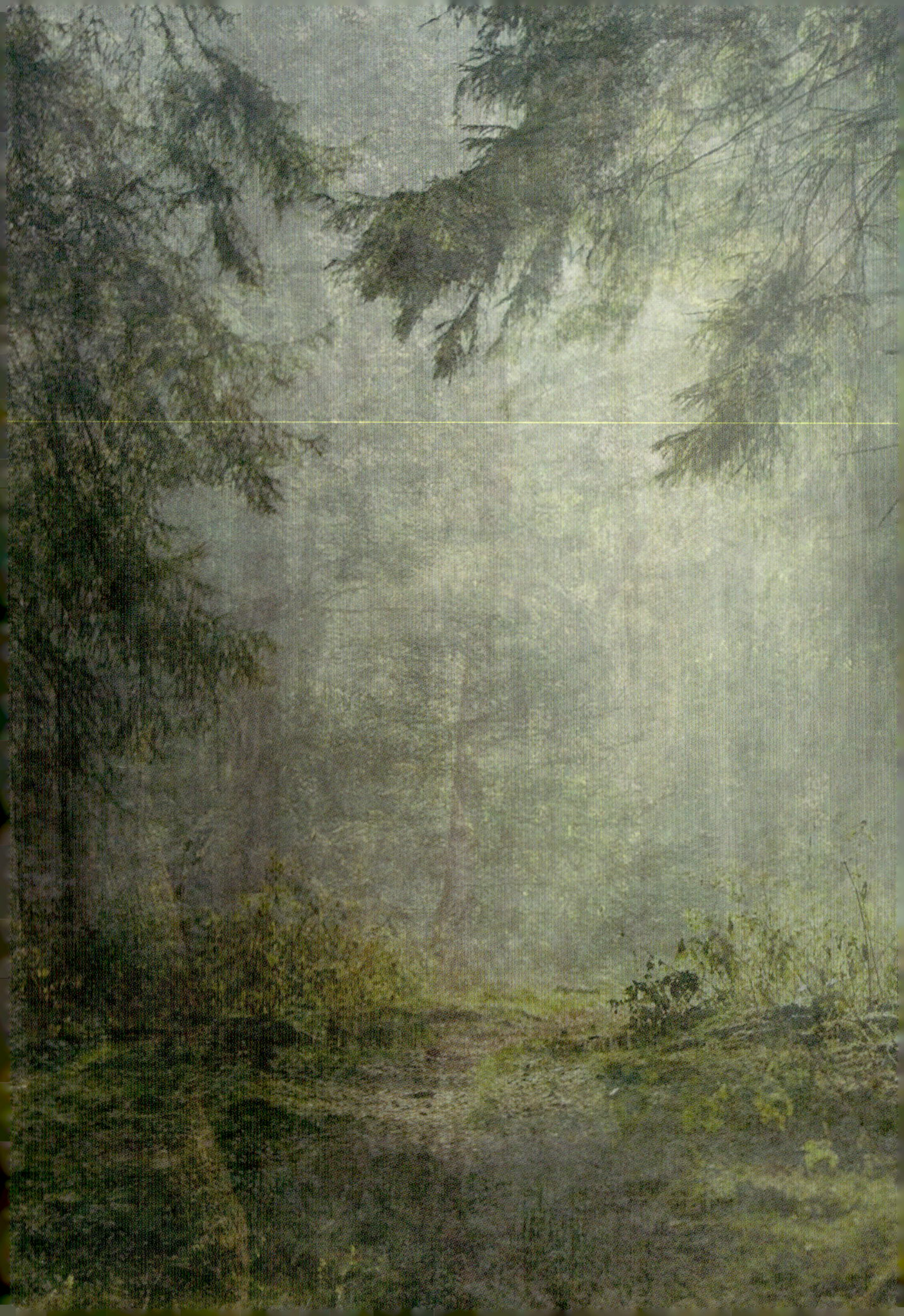

PHOTO CREDITS

Pages 11–13: Courtesy of the artist, Maria Kokunova

Pages 14–17: Courtesy Klaus von Nichtssagend Gallery, New York and Park View / Paul Soto, Los Angeles

Page 19: Glenda Lissette

Page 20: Courtesy of the artist, © Isabelle Wenzel

Pages 23–25: Kate Peters

Pages 27–29: Courtesy of the artist, Maria Katayama

Page 30: Courtesy of the artist, DOCUMENT, Chicago, and Vielmetter Los Angeles

Page 33: Courtesy of the artist, Cassils

Pages 34, 36–37: Courtesy of the artist, Cara Phillips

Pages 38, 40–41: Courtesy of the artist, Maija Tammi

Pages 45–47: Ana Zibelnik

Page 48: Courtesy of The Estate of Khadija Saye

Page 51: © David Avazzadeh, 2019

Pages 52, 54–55: Alys Tomlinson

Page 57: Courtesy of the artist, Pawel Jaszczuk

Pages 58, 60–61: © Marwan Bassiouni from the series Prayer Rug Selfies

Page 63: Courtesy of the artist, Kristine Potter

Page 65: Murray Ballard

Pages 69–71: Lindley Warren Mickunas

Page 72: © 2017 Masaki Yamamoto, courtesy of Zen Foto Gallery

Pages 75–77: Courtesy of the artist, Jonny Briggs

Pages 78, 80–81: Courtesy of the artist, Pixy Liao

Page 83: © Luis Alberto Rodriguez 2021, courtesy Loose Joints

Pages 84–87: Andres Gonzalez

Pages 88, 90–91: © George Georgiou

Page 92: Courtesy of the artist, Jack Davison (Alexandra, 2020, part of a series of portraits for the *New York Time Magazine* issue "What We've Learned in Quarantine," 2020)

Page 95: Courtesy of the artist, Deanna Dikeman

Page 99: Courtesy of the artist, Laurence Rasti

Page 100: © Zanele Muholi. Courtesy of the artist, Yancey Richardson Gallery, New York, and Stevenson Gallery, Cape Town and Johannesburg

Page 103: Courtesy of Library Street Collective and Sutton Comms

Pages 104, 106–107: Courtesy of the artist, Guanyu Xu, and Yancey Richardson Gallery, New York

Page 109: Courtesy of the artist, Keyezua

Page 110: David Castillo Gallery

Pages 113, 114–115: Ryan Debolski, LIKE (Gnomic Book, 2020)

Page 117: Courtesy of the artist, Doug Rickard

Page 121: Lindsay Godin

Pages 122–125: Courtesy Peter Funch and V1 Gallery

Page 127: Adji Dieye

Page 128: © Silvia Rosi, Courtesy of the artist

Page 131: Courtesy of the artist and Klowden Mann Gallery

Page 132: Abdo Shanan

Pages 135–137: Clément Lambelet

Pages 138, 140–141: Amy Elkins

ACKNOWLEDGMENTS

I would like to extend a gargantuan thank-you to the following people whose experience, creativity, and insight helped
to shape this book. To my editor, Michael Sand, and the
design and editorial team at Abrams: Diane Shaw, Deb Wood,
Elizabeth Broussard, and Glenn Ramirez. Thank you to my kind
and supremely talented personal editor, Riley Johnson, for
his ongoing and thoughtful comments, and to my agent and
voice of reason, Katherine Cowles. Image research was under-
taken by the unstoppable Kim Hungerford and Jack Harries of
RAFT, and further thanks go to Yana Wernicke, James Bryant,
Selwyn Leamy, Caitlin Walsh, Dan Golden, Lukasz Pruchnik,
and Danielle Mourning. And, of course, thank you to all the
photographers who generously contributed work and so gra-
ciously tolerated my working methods that were, at times, a
touch chaotic.

Editor: Michael Sand
Managing Editor: Glenn Ramirez
Designer: Diane Shaw
Design Manager: Shawn Dahl, dahlimama inc
Production Manager: Kathleen Gaffney

Library of Congress Control Number: 2021932502

ISBN: 978-1-4197-5145-5
eISBN: 978-1-64700-569-6

Text copyright © 2021 Henry Carroll
Photograph credits on page 142
Image research: Kim Hungerford & Jack Harries (rafteditions.com)

Cover © 2021 Abrams
Front cover photograph: Courtesy of the artist, Maria Kokunova

Printed and bound in the United States
10 9 8 7 6 5 4 3 2 1

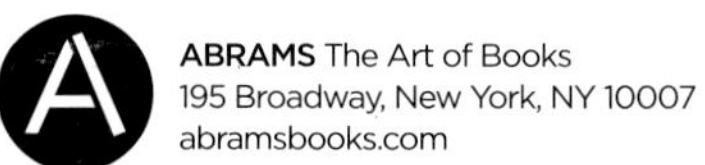
ABRAMS The Art of Books
195 Broadway, New York, NY 10007
abramsbooks.com